THE WHITES
OF THEIR EYES

The Public Square Book Series

PRINCETON UNIVERSITY PRESS
Ruth O'Brien, Series Editor

THE WHITES OF THEIR EYES

The Tea Party's Revolution and the Battle over American History

JILL LEPORE

PRINCETON UNIVERSITY PRESS
PRINCETON AND OXFORD

Published by Princeton University Press,
41 William Street, Princeton, New Jersey 08540
In the United Kingdom: Princeton University Press,
6 Oxford Street, Woodstock, Oxfordshire OX20 1TW
press.princeton.edu
All Rights Reserved

Library of Congress Cataloging-in-Publication Data

Lepore, Jill, 1966–
    The whites of their eyes : the Tea Party's revolution and the
battle over American history / Jill Lepore.
        p. cm. — (The public square book series)
    Includes bibliographical references and index.
    ISBN 978-0-691-15027-7 (hardcover : acid-free paper)
    1. United States—History—Philosophy. 2. United
States—Historiography—Social aspects. 3. United
States—Historiography—Political aspects. 4. United States—
History—Revolution, 1775–1783—Influence. 5. United States—
History—Errors, inventions, etc. 6. Tea Party movement.
7. Fundamentalism—United States. 8. Evangelicalism—United
States. 9. Right-wing extremists—United States. I. Title.
    E175.9.L46 2010
    973.3'115—dc22

                                                    2010030251

British Library Cataloging-in-Publication Data is available

Parts of this book were originally published in *The New Yorker*.

The spelling, capitalization, and punctuation of eighteenth-century
writing have been left, whenever possible, as they were in the original.

This book has been composed in Sabon
Printed on acid-free paper. ∞
Printed in the United States of America

10 9 8 7 6 5 4 3 2 1

To my sons

I do not mean to say, that the scenes of the revolution
are now or *ever will be* entirely forgotten;
But that, like everything else, they must fade
upon the memory of the world, and grow
more and more dim by the lapse of time.

—Abraham Lincoln, 1838

CONTENTS

FOREWORD

Ruth O'Brien

Recalling the soldiers at Bunker Hill who, facing the British, were told to get close enough to see "the whites of their eyes," Jill Lepore's magnificent book takes a very close look at both the founding of the United States and its legacy—the unending battle over American history. In artful and vivid prose, Lepore takes readers the distance between past and present, and then back again, sometimes all in the space of a page, to explain, for instance, how the Revolution could spawn both the conservative Tea Party, in the twenty-first century, and its ideological opposite—the liberal Tax Equity for Americans (TEA) Party, in the 1970s and, finally, to offer a thoughtful meditation on history itself. The study of history, she argues, is always "controversial, contentious, and contested," but the Tea Party's Revolution was antihistorical, tangling together originalism, evangelicalism, and fundamentalism. Lepore, deftly navigating between history, culture, and politics, also offers a caution about her own profession. In the 1970s, she argues, academic historians belittled the Bicentennial as "schlock" but "didn't offer an answer, a story, to a country that needed one." "That left plenty of room," she suggests, "for a lot of other people to get into the history business." And they did.

Beginning in 2009, one month after the election of Barack Obama, the Tea Party charged the new administration with imposing "taxation without representation," as if health care legislation, passed by Congress in 2010, were like the Stamp Act, imposed by Parliament in 1765. Lepore shows us, though, that this kind of maneuver was not new. "Americans have drawn Revolutionary analogies before," she writes. "They have drawn them for a very long time." To reveal how historians think about the past, Lepore carries readers on a journey, her journey, as she scrambles onto a replica Revolutionary ship, sits in dimly lit Revolutionary taverns, and attends Revolutionary reenactments. By musing on how the past can better inform the present and on how historians might play a civic role, this book enters the public arena—and the Public Square.

THE WHITES
OF THEIR EYES

PROLOGUE

Party Like It's 1773

One morning last March,
I pressed against the new barbed and galvanized
fence on the Boston Common.
    —Robert Lowell, "For the Union Dead," 1960

Lashed to a dock in the oldest working shipyard in America, the Boston Tea Party Ship, or what was left of her, sat in a dozen feet of brackish water in Gloucester Harbor. I went to see her one raw winter's morning in March. Her bones creaked when the wind blew, but no halyards clanged: she had no masts, no rigging, and hardly any decking. She was not open to the public. To clamber aboard, I had to climb down an iron ladder, cross two floating docks, crawl under a stretch of ropes, and walk a plank, barefoot. Topsides, it felt like being inside a greenhouse, if a greenhouse were a houseboat and haunted: plastic sheeting stapled to a tented frame of two-by-fours sheltered the ship from gale, sleet, rain, snow, and every other act of God to afflict the rocky coast of Cape Ann, the site of twenty-seven shipwrecks before John Hancock convinced the Massachusetts legislature to raise money to build a pair of lighthouses, whose whale-oil lights were first lit on December 21, 1771, Forefathers Day, a holiday commemorating the arrival of the *Mayflower*'s first landing party in Plymouth, a century and a half before.[1] Americans love an anniversary.

Beaver was the name carved, ornately, in her stern. She was a replica. No one knows what became of the original *Beaver*, one of three ships whose cargo of East India Company tea was dumped into Boston Harbor on December 16, 1773, which pleased Hancock, who had been making a great deal of money by smuggling Dutch tea into the colonies. That *Beaver* was long gone; like many another old boat, she sank or burned or was junked for parts, a derelict on a distant shore. In 1972, three Boston businessmen got the idea of sailing a ship across the Atlantic for the tea party's bicentennial. They bought a Baltic schooner, built in Denmark in 1908, and had her rerigged as an English brig, powered by an anachronistic engine that was, unfortunately, put in backwards and caught fire on the way over. Still, she made it to Boston in time for the hoopla. After that, the bicentennial *Beaver* was anchored at the Congress Street Bridge, next to what became the Boston Children's Museum. For years, it was a popular attraction. In 2001, though, the site was struck by lightning and closed for repairs. A renovation was planned. But that was stalled by the Big Dig, the excavation of three and a half miles of tunnel designed to rescue the city from the blight of Interstate 93, an elevated expressway that, since the 1950s, had made it almost impossible to see the ocean, and this in a city whose earliest maps were inked with names like Flounder Lane, Sea Street, and Dock Square. (Boston is, and always has been, a fishy place.) In 2007, welders working on the Congress Street Bridge accidentally started another fire, although by then, the *Beaver* had already been towed, by tugboat, twenty-eight miles to Gloucester, where she'd been ever since, bereft, abandoned, and all but forgotten.[2]

On the day I went to Gloucester, the *Beaver* was a skeleton, a ghost ship, but the Tea Party was the talk of the nation.

It had started on February 19, 2009, one month after the inauguration of a new president, Barack Obama. Rick Santelli, a business commentator on a CNBC morning news and talk show called *Squawk Box*, was outraged by the economic policies of the new administration. "This is America!" he hollered from a trading room floor in Chicago, surrounded by cheering commodities brokers. "How many of you people want to pay for your neighbor's mortgage?" He was sure about one thing: "If you read our Founding Fathers, people like Benjamin Franklin and Jefferson, what we're doing in this country now is making them roll over in their graves." He wanted to dump some derivative securities in Lake Michigan. He wanted a new tea party.[3]

Within hours, Santelli's call to arms was dubbed "the rant heard round the world," a reference to a poem written by Ralph Waldo Emerson in 1836—

Here once the embattled farmers stood
And fired the shot heard round the world

—on the occasion of the erection of a statue memorializing the men (including Emerson's grandfather) who faced the British in Concord in 1775.[4] Almost overnight, Tea Parties sprang up across the country. The Chicago Tea Party adopted the motto "Revolution Is Brewing."[5]

On April 15, Tax Day, the day Americans file their income tax returns, Tea Party protests were held in hundreds of cities and towns. Everywhere, people told stories about the Revolution. On Boston Common, a gently sloping patch of grass set aside for pastureland in 1634, four years after Puritans founded their city on a hill, state senator Robert Hedlund, a Republican from Plymouth County, addressed a few hundred people gathered around a tree. "The history books in our public schools," he said, had failed to teach that what happened in 1773 "was about a collection of interested citizens afraid of seeing their economic success determined by the whim of an interventionist governmental body."[6] Michael Johns of the Heritage Foundation, believing that the United States was founded as a Christian nation, wanted to send this message to the White House:

> Mr. Obama, every historical document signed in Philadelphia, every founding document in this nation, has cited our creator. That is the basis on which we distinguish ourselves in the world. And it is the foundation of our liberty and our God-given freedom.

David Tuerck, an economist from Suffolk University, wore a George Washington tie: "In case there are any people here with Obama's picture in their living room, they can see what a real patriot looks like." The problem wasn't just in DC, Tuerck said. "Right here in Massachusetts, we have a Supreme Judicial Court that thinks it can redefine marriage without a thought to the will of the people." (In 2004, same-sex marriage became legal in Massachusetts when the state's highest court ruled that its restriction was unconstitutional.) "It's time for us to rally around a new cause," Tuerck said, "which is to return America to the principles for which our forefathers fought and died. It's time for a new American Revolution. And I can think of no better place to start that revolution than right here."

Shawni Littlehale from Smart Girl Politics agreed. "Two hundred and thirty-three years ago," she said, "the silent majority got together in Boston, fed up with taxation without representation, and held a tea party." (The silent majority did no such thing. "Silent majority" used to be a euphemism for the dead. The phrase's meaning didn't change until about 1969, when Richard Nixon used it to refer to Americans who, he believed, quietly supported the Vietnam War.)[7] Kris Mineau, an evangelical minister who heads the Massachusetts Family Institute, invoked the sage of Monticello: "I want to give you all a little history lesson. Thomas Jefferson, our third president, from that Oval Office, he wrote, 'It is only in the love of one's own family that heartfelt happiness is known.'" (Given the Hemingses, Jefferson's children by Sally Hemings, one of his slaves, this was a particularly striking choice.)[8] Wearing colonial garb from head to toe was a Pentecostal minister named Paul Jehle, executive director of the Plymouth Rock Foundation, an organization founded in 1970, on the occasion of the 350th anniversary of the *Mayflower*'s voyage, "to preserve, rehearse and propagate the rich Christian heritage of the United States of America, beginning with the Pilgrims." Jehle preached that "God gives rights; governments don't" and urged people to form something like Bible study groups: "Our little organization, Plymouth Rock Foundation, we publish materials, where you can study the Constitution line by line, from its original intent, and what was meant by the founders. You can study in small groups. You can study all kinds of things, because we need to reeducate ourselves, because the present education system won't."

Elsewhere, activists stapled Lipton tea bags to their hats, like so many fishing lures. "Party Like It's 1773" read one sign.[9] Newt Gingrich spoke at a Tea Party in New York. In Atlanta, where Fox News celebrity Sean Hannity broadcast from a rally attended by some fifteen thousand people, the show opened with a white-wigged reenactor dressed as an eighteenth-century minister—black great coat, ruffled white shirt—who, in front of a backdrop of the Constitution and a flag of thirteen stars, said, before introducing "Citizen Sean Hannity": "The United States of America was formed by common people, risking all they had to defy an arrogant regime, taxing them into submission. And now that arrogance has returned, threatening the very foundation of our republic. My name is Thomas Paine."[10] (I guess this wasn't the same Paine as the man who wrote, "All national institutions of churches, whether Jewish, Christian, or Turkish, appear to me no other than human inventions, set up to terrify and enslave mankind, and monopolise power and profit.")[11] In Washington, someone threw a box of tea bags over the fence that surrounds the White House. All over the country, people turned up wearing tricorns and periwigs, cuffed shirts and kersey waistcoats, knee breeches and buckled shoes, dressing as the founders, quoting the founders, waving copies of the Constitution, arguing that the time for revolution had come again.[12]

At the time, I happened to be teaching an undergraduate seminar on the American Revolution at Harvard, reading monographs and articles in scholarly journals; visiting archives; transcribing letters and diaries; touring graveyards and museums; and grading papers on the Stamp Act, the Boston Massacre, the Intolerable Acts, the Battle of Lexington and Concord, the Siege of Boston, and the Battle of Bunker Hill. Meanwhile, at home, my nine-year-old was busy memorizing Henry Wadsworth Longfellow's 1860 poem, "Paul Revere's Ride," an assignment given, every year, by a masterful teacher in a public school in Cambridge, arguably the most liberal city in the most liberal state in the nation. In my house, we couldn't sit down for dinner without one or another of the under-tens clearing his throat and reciting

Listen, my children, and you shall hear
Of the midnight ride of Paul Revere,

On the eighteenth of April, in Seventy-five;
Hardly a man is now alive
Who remembers that famous day and year.[13]

Every generation tells its own story about what the Revolution was about, of course, since no one is alive who remembers it anymore. But the Tea Party's Revolution wasn't just another generation's story—it was more like a reenactment—and its complaint about taxation without representation followed the inauguration of a president who won the electoral vote 365 to 173 and earned 53 percent of the popular vote. In an age of universal suffrage, the citizenry could hardly be said to lack representation. Nationwide, voter turnout, in November of 2008, was 57 percent, the highest since Nixon was elected in 1968.[14] Something more was going on, something not about taxation or representation but about history itself. It wasn't only that the Tea Party's version of American history bore almost no resemblance to the Revolution I study and teach. That was true, but it wasn't new. People who study the Revolution have almost always found the speeches people make about it to be something other than "true history." In 1841, George Ticknor Curtis, a Boston lawyer and constitutional historian, wrote *The True Uses of American Revolutionary History*. He was hopping mad about the tea partiers of his day. "The age for declamation about the American Revolution has passed away," he insisted. He was sick of people invoking the Revolution to advance a cause. He didn't want to be misunderstood, though. "Do I propose to forget the past? Would I cut loose from the great sheet-anchor of our destiny, and send the political and social system to drift over the wide waters of a boundless future, or on the turbulent waves of the present, careless of the great dead, their principles, their deeds, their renown, their splendid illustration of the great truths of man's political and social state?"[15] No. He just wished people would study the Revolution instead of using it to make political arguments. Curtis called this kind of thing declamation. The word "blather" also comes to mind. What was curious about the Tea Party's Revolution, though, was that it wasn't just kooky history; it was *anti*history. In May of 2009, a month after the Tea Party's first Tax Day protests, Hannity began lecturing about the Sons of Liberty. "In 1765, Parliament passed the Stamp Act," he said on his show one day. He told of the protests under the Liberty Tree, in Boston. Then he unveiled a new Fox News graphic: a liberty tree.

> In the spirit of our Founding Fathers, with our liberties once again threatened, we introduce our own Liberty Tree. Now as you can see, our tree is built upon the roots of life, liberty, pursuit of happiness, and freedom. They support the trunk of the tree, which is made of we the people. And the trunk supports the branches and the fruits of our liberty represented by the apples. It is those apples, the fruits of our liberty, that this administration is now picking clean.

He concluded, "It took more than two hundred years, but it now looks like we are headed back to where we started."[16]

In antihistory, time is an illusion. Either we're there, two hundred years ago, or they're here, among us. When Congress began debating an overhaul of the health care system, this, apparently, was very distressing to the Founding Fathers. "The founders are here today," said John Ridpath of the Ayn Rand Institute, at a Boston Tea Party rally on the Common on the Fourth of July. "They're all around us."[17]

To the far right, everything about Barack Obama and his administration seemed somehow alarming, as if his election had ripped a tear in the fabric of time. In August, the Department of Education announced that the president would be making a speech addressed to the nation's schoolchildren, about what a good idea it is to stay in school and to study hard. The speech would be made available to public schools, on C-SPAN, educational channels, and the White House's website. Jim Greer, then chairman of the Republican Party of Florida, said: "As the father of four children, I am absolutely appalled that taxpayer dollars are being used to spread President Obama's socialist ideology." Hannity said, "It seems very close to indoctrination." A pundit named Michelle Malkin, appearing as a guest on Hannity's show, added, "The left has always used kids in public schools as guinea pigs and as junior lobbyists for their social liberal agenda." Glenn Beck, a former talk-radio host who launched a show on Fox News the day before Obama was inaugurated, compared the president to Mussolini. Some schools refused to show the speech. Some parents kept their kids home that day. Here is the pith of the speech they missed: "No matter what you want to do with your life," Obama said, "I guarantee that you'll need an education to do it."[18]

That fall, a little-known Massachusetts Republican state senator named Scott Brown launched a campaign for the U.S. Senate seat vacated by the death of Ted Kennedy, who had held it since 1962. Kennedy had been a staunch advocate of health care reform. Brown pledged to defeat passage of the health care bill. In a special election held on January 19, 2010, Brown defeated the Democrat, Massachusetts attorney general Martha Coakley, by a seven-point margin, a victory for which the Tea Party took credit. Fox News called Brown's triumph the "Massachusetts Massacre," a reference, I guess, to the Boston Massacre, although what the 2010 election and the 1770 shooting share begins and ends with the word "massacre."

On February 18, 2010, a fifty-three-year-old software engineer named Joseph Andrew Stark set fire to his house and then flew a one-engine plane into an office building in Austin, Texas, where some two hundred IRS employees work, killing himself and an IRS manager, a man with six children. In a suicide note that Stark posted on the Internet the morning he died, he wrote,

> Sadly, starting at early ages we in this country have been brainwashed to believe that, in return for our dedication and service, our government stands for justice for all. We are further brainwashed to believe that there is freedom in this place, and that we should be ready to lay our lives down for the noble principles represented by its founding fathers. Remember? One of these was "no taxation without representation." I have spent the total years of my adulthood unlearning that crap from only a few years of my childhood.

Stark, who had been feuding with the IRS for years, had no connection to any political organization. He was not a Tea Partier. He was alone and adrift, but he also seems to have been caught up in something, something bitter and terrible, about the Founding Fathers and about innocence lost.[19]

On March 5, 2010, the 240th anniversary of the Boston Massacre, Glenn Beck issued a special Fox News report on "Indoctrination in America": "Tonight, America, I want you to sit down and talk to your kids and hold your kids close to you," he began. "Get the kids out of this indoctrination or our republic will be lost." He was talking about environmentalism and about a lot of other things, too: "Our kids are being brainwashed with the concept of—I've shown it to you before, earth worship. Earth worship. I pledge allegiance to the earth. Social justice. What is social justice? God is being eliminated from the equation entirely." He found occasion to reach back to the Revolution: "Let me give you the words of George Washington, 'It is impossible to rightly govern a nation without God and the Bible.'" Like Hannity, Beck had begun giving history lessons. He outfitted his studio with chalk and a blackboard and even old-fashioned oak school chairs and desks, as if from a one-room schoolhouse. What our children are learning, Beck warned, darkly, is nothing short of learn-to-hate-America lunacy.[20]

That was a Friday. The next morning, I rode a rumbling Red Line subway car from Cambridge, over the Charles, a river named after a king, to watch the annual reenactment of the Boston Massacre, in front of the Old State House, built in 1713, the oldest public building in the United States.[21] A scrum of rambunctious kids jostled for position on a narrow and cramped walkway along the brick building's southern face. A burly British Army reenactor playing Captain Thomas Preston recruited ten grenadiers, outfitting them with gold-rimmed tricornered hats, brass-buttoned red coats, and wooden muskets. He lined them up and, feigning sternness, commanded his pint-sized soldiers to shout, "God save the king!"

They giggled.

Preston glared at them. He growled. "Would you rather be French?"

"My mom speaks French!" said Isaac Doherty, a six-year-old from Quincy.

"I know karate!" another kid piped up.

Then they all started clobbering each other with their muskets.

Preston sighed.

A National Park Service ranger handed out Styrofoam balls to the rest of the kids in the crowd who, gleefully playing an angry mob, hurled the fake snowballs at the soldiers.

"Bloody redcoats!"

"Go back to England!

"Stinking lobsterbacks!"

Every year, this gets a little out of hand. Madeline Raynor, age ten, got pelted in the eye. It looked like it smarted. She took it in stride. "I learned it's really hard to be a Redcoat," she told a reporter from the *Boston Globe*.[22] I decided I wasn't worried about anyone getting indoctrinated.

The next week, in Austin, the Texas School Board convened to discuss amendments to the state's social studies curriculum. A review of the curriculum, from kindergarten through high school, had been under way for some time. It made national news because of its national implications. The state of Texas is one of the largest buyers of textbooks in the country; its standards wield considerable influence, nationwide, on publishers' content, since publishers do not generally provide different editions for different states.[23] Conservative board members, who, during an earlier revision of the state's science curriculum, had fought for the teaching of creationism, stated their belief that liberals had contaminated the teaching of American history. "I reject the notion by the left of a constitutional separation of church and state," said one board member, a real estate agent, who added, "I have $1,000 for the charity of your choice if you can find it in the Constitution."[24]

Beginning with the rise of the New Left in the 1960s, women's history, labor history, and the history of slavery and emancipation—the study, in one way or another, of ordinary people, of groups, and, especially, of conflict—dominated the academic study of American history. (Every school subject is taught differently than it was in the 1950s, and American history is no exception.) In word-by-word amendments to the existing curriculum, the Texas School Board proposed rejecting this scholarship, replacing "ordinary people" with "patriots and good citizens"; dispensing with "capitalism" in favor of "free enterprise"; and calling the "slave trade" the "Atlantic triangular trade." The amendments also included some striking adjustments to the teaching of twentieth-century history: a defense of McCarthyism, for instance (in studying the House Committee on Un-American Activities, students were to be responsible for explaining "how the later release of the Venona Papers confirmed suspicions of communist infiltration in U.S. government"), and an emphasis on "the conservative resurgence of the 1980s and 1990s, including Phyllis Schlafly, the Contract with America, the Heritage Foundation, the Moral Majority, and the National Rifle Association." But what proved most controversial, as the press picked up the story, were changes to the teaching of the founding era of American history. Thomas Aquinas was added to a list of thinkers who inspired the American Revolution; Thomas Jefferson (who once wrote about a "wall of separation between Church & State") was removed. The United States, called, in the old curriculum, a "democratic society," was now to be referred to as a "constitutional republic." Biblical law was to be studied as an intellectual influence on the Declaration of Independence, the Articles of Confederation, and the Constitution. Kids in Texas, who used to study Locke, Hobbes, and Montesquieu as thinkers whose ideas informed the nation's founding, would now dispense with Hobbes, in favor of Moses.[25]

The week the Texas School Board was meeting in Austin, a chapter of the Tea Party was holding its regular monthly meeting in Boston. I decided to go. In the weeks that followed, I went to more Tea Party meetings and rallies. I also visited historic sites, places I'd been many times before, and interviewed museum curators, people I'd known, and worked with, for years. Meanwhile, I dug in the archives. And I drove up to Gloucester. Reading, watching, listening, and even scrambling over that ship, I came to believe, and this book argues, that the use of the Revolution by the far right had quite a lot to do with the *Beaver*, which sailed across the Atlantic, nearly sank on the way over, and dropped anchor in Boston Harbor just in time for Watergate, at a moment in American history when no one could agree on what story a country torn apart by war in Vietnam and civil rights strife at home ought to tell about its unruly beginnings.

This book also makes an argument about the American political tradition: nothing trumps the Revolution. From the start, the Tea Party's chief political asset was its name: the echo of the Revolution conferred upon a scattered, diffuse, and confused movement a degree of legitimacy and the appearance, almost, of coherence. Aside from the name and the costume, the Tea Party offered an analogy: rejecting the bailout is like dumping the tea; health care reform is like the Tea Act; our struggle is like theirs. Americans have drawn Revolutionary analogies before. They have drawn them for a very long time. When in doubt, in American politics, left, right, or center, deploy the Founding Fathers. Relying on this sort of analogy, advocates of health care reform could have insisted that, since John Hancock once urged the Massachusetts legislature to raise funds for the erection of lighthouses, he would have supported state health care reform, because, like a lighthouse, health care coverage concerns public safety. That might sound strained, at best, but something quite like it has been tried. In 1798, John Adams signed an "Act for the relief of sick and disabled Seamen": state and later federal government officials collected taxes from shipmasters, which were used to build hospitals and provide medical care for merchant and naval seamen. In the 1940s, health care reformers used this precedent to bolster their case. Government-sponsored health care wasn't un-American, these reformers argued; Adams had thought of it.[26]

That political tradition is long-standing. But the more I looked at the Tea Party, at Beck and Hannity as history teachers, and at the Texas School Board reforms, the more it struck me that the statement at the core of the far right's version of American history went just a bit further. It was more literal than an analogy. It wasn't "our struggle is like theirs." It was "we are there" or "they are here." The unanswered question of the Bicentennial was, "What ails the American spirit?" Antihistory has no patience for ambiguity, self-doubt, and introspection. The Tea Party had an answer: "We have forsaken the Founding Fathers." Political affiliates are, by nature, motley. But what the Tea Party, Beck and Hannity, and the Texas School Board shared was a set of assumptions about the relationship between the past and the present that was both broadly anti-intellectual and, quite specifically, antihistorical, not least because it defies chronology, the logic of time.[27] To say that we are there, or the Founding Fathers are here, or that we have forsaken them and they're rolling over in their graves because of the latest, breaking political development—the election of the United States' first African American president, for instance—is to subscribe to a set of assumptions about the relationship between the past and the present stricter, even, than the strictest form of constitutional originalism, a set of assumptions that, conflating originalism, evangelicalism, and heritage tourism, amounts to a variety of fundamentalism.

Historical fundamentalism is marked by the belief that a particular and quite narrowly defined past—"the founding"— is ageless and sacred and to be worshipped; that certain historical texts—"the founding documents"—are to be read in the same spirit with which religious fundamentalists read, for instance, the Ten Commandments; that the Founding Fathers were divinely inspired; that the academic study of history (whose standards of evidence and methods of analysis are based on skepticism) is a conspiracy and, furthermore, blasphemy; and that political arguments grounded in appeals to the founding documents, as sacred texts, and to the Founding Fathers, as prophets, are therefore incontrovertible.[28]

The past haunts us all. Just how is a subject of this book. But time moves forward, not backward. Chronology is like gravity. Nothing falls up. We cannot go back to the eighteenth century, and the Founding Fathers are not, in fact, here with us today. They weren't even called the Founding Fathers until Warren G. Harding coined that phrase in his keynote address at the Republican National Convention in 1916. Harding also invoked the Founding Fathers during his inauguration in 1921—"Standing in this presence, mindful of the solemnity of this occasion, feeling the emotions which no one may know until he senses the great weight of responsibility for himself, I must utter my belief in the divine inspiration of the founding fathers"—in what is quite possibly the worst inaugural address ever written. ("It reminds me of a string of wet sponges," H. L. Mencken wrote. "It reminds me of tattered washing on the line; it reminds me of stale bean soup, of college yells, of dogs barking idiotically through endless nights. It is so bad that a sort of grandeur creeps into it.")[29] The Founding Fathers haven't been rolling over in their graves for very long, either. Not one was roused from his eternal slumber with any regularity until about the time that Harding called the founders our fathers (and, more particularly, his) and said they were divinely inspired (which had the curious effect of granting to his presidency something akin to the divine right of kings). Dead presidents and deceased delegates to the Constitutional Convention only first got restless in 1868, in a play called *The Spirit of Seventy-Six*, published in Boston and set in a fictitious, suffragette future, where women voting and holding office were said to be "enough to make George Washington turn in his grave!"[30]

If that sounds old-fashioned, that's because it is; we don't say that people turn in their graves anymore. We say they "roll over." That expression came into use in 1883, the year after Ralph Waldo Emerson died.[31] Maybe it was Emerson who was rolling over in his grave. In American history, all roads lead to the Revolution: if Emerson had rolled over in his grave (miffed about the "rant heard round the world"), that would have to have happened in Concord's Sleepy Hollow, a cemetery over whose dedication Emerson presided in 1855, calling it a "garden for the living," and where he was buried in 1882; Sleepy Hollow borrows its name from a story written by Washington Irving, who, born in 1783, the year the Treaty of Paris was signed, was named after George Washington; "The Legend of Sleepy Hollow," published in 1820, is set in 1790 in a town haunted by the ghost of a Hessian soldier who had his head blown off, by cannonball, during some "nameless battle during the Revolutionary War":

Certain of the most authentic historians of those parts, who have been careful in collecting and collating the floating facts concerning this spectre, allege that the body of the trooper having been buried in the churchyard, the ghost rides forth to the scene of battle in nightly quest of his head, and that the rushing speed with which he sometimes passes along the Hollow, like a midnight blast, is owing to his being belated, and in a hurry to get back to the churchyard before daybreak.[32]

I'd have worried about Emerson, wriggling, rotted, and miserable in his worm-ridden coffin in Sleepy Hollow, except that, of course, people don't roll over in their graves any more than headless horsemen ride forth through the night. Emerson rests, undisturbed. But the battle over the Revolution rages on.

This book is an account of that battle, over the centuries. It is also, along the way, a history of the Revolution—an archival investigation into the relationship between the people and their rulers, between liberty and slavery, between learning and ignorance, and between irreverence and deference. Each of this book's five chapters is set in one place—Boston—but each travels through time: each begins with the rise of the Tea Party, in 2009 and 2010; moves backward to iconic moments in the coming of the American Revolution, in the 1760s and 1770s; and then skips forward to the Bicentennial of those events, in the 1960s and 1970s. Just as faith has its demands and its solaces, there are, I believe, demands and solaces in the study of history.[33] My point in telling three stories at once is not to ignore the passage of time but rather to dwell on it, to see what's remembered and what's forgotten, what's kept and what's lost.

Standing on the *Beaver* watching sea-weedy waves slap the ship's hull, I thought about how sailors on ocean-faring vessels once measured depth. They would drop a rope weighted with lead into the water and let it plummet till it reached bottom. I like to sink lines, too, to get to the bottom of things. This book is an argument against historical fundamentalism. It makes that argument by measuring the distance between the past and the present. It measures that distance by taking soundings in the ocean of time. Here, now, we float on a surface of yesterdays. Below swirls the blue-green of childhood. Deeper still is the obscurity of long ago. But the eighteenth century, oh, the eighteenth century lies fathoms down.

CHAPTER 1

Ye Olde Media

CONTAINING REFLECTIONS ON NATIONS FOUNDED IN
REVOLUTIONS—AN INTRODUCTION TO OUR CHARACTERS—A
HISTORY OF THE STAMP ACT—THE BIRTH, DEATH, AND
RESURRECTION OF THE NEWSPAPER—ITS DIRE FATE, OF
LATE—AND A VISIT TO THE GREEN DRAGON TAVERN

"Everybody, anywhere I go, always asks me, 'Where did you get that hat?'" Austin Hess told me, when we first met, beside a statue of Samuel Adams in front of Faneuil Hall. Hess, a twenty-six-year-old engineer and member of the steering committee of the Boston Tea Party, was wearing a tricornered hat: not your ordinary felt-and-cardboard fake but the genuine article, wide-brimmed and raffish. In April of 2009, two months after Rick Santelli, outraged by the Obama administration's stimulus package, called for a new tea party, Hess showed up at a Tax Day rally on the Boston Common. He was carrying a sign that read "I Can Stimulate Myself." He was much photographed; he appeared on television, a local Fox affiliate. He was wearing his hat. He got it at Plimoth Plantation. It was made of "distressed faux leather." You could order it on-line. It was called the Scallywag.[1]

The importance of the American Revolution to the twenty-first-century Tea Party movement might seem to have been slight—as if the name were mere happenstance, the knee

breeches knickknacks, the rhetoric of revolution unthinking—
but that was not entirely the case, especially in Boston, where
the local chapter of the Tea Party bore a particular burden: it
happened here. "Everybody in the movement is interested in
the Revolution," Hess told me. He took his debt to the founders seriously: "We believe that we are carrying on their tradition, and if they were around today, they would be in the
streets with us, leading us, and they'd be even angrier than
we are. I imagine we'd have to politely ask them to leave their
muskets at home."[2]

"Who shall write the history of the American revolution?" John Adams once asked Thomas Jefferson. "Who can
write it? Who will ever be able to write it?" "Nobody," was
Jefferson's reply. "The life and soul of history must forever
remain unknown."[3] The records were murky, the course of
events astonishing, the consequences immeasurable. Nobody
could write the history of the Revolution, but everyone would
have to try; it was too important not to. There was also this
dilemma: a nation born in revolution will always eye its history warily, and with anxiety. It's good that it happened
once; twice could be trouble. The Revolution's first historian,
Peter Oliver, was a Loyalist from Boston. Consumed by bit-
terness, regret, and rancor, he wrote the "Origin & Progress
of the American Rebellion" in 1781, from exile in England.
He didn't think the Revolution should have happened even
once.[4] The first patriot historian of the Revolution, David
Ramsay, a physician who had been a delegate to the Continental Congress from South Carolina and whose two-volume
history was published in 1789, stated the problem as well as
anyone. "The right of the people to resist their rulers, when
invading their liberties, forms the corner stone of the American republic," Ramsay wrote in *The History of the American*

Revolution, but "this principle, though just in itself, is not favourable to the tranquility of present establishments."[5] Ramsay appreciated the acuteness of the difficulty: celebrating the birth of the nation, and carrying on in its spirit, risked promoting still more revolution, unrest, impermanence, and instability, when what the new nation needed was calm. "A little rebellion, now and then, is a good thing," Jefferson wrote from Paris in 1786, on hearing word of Shays's Rebellion, an armed uprising by farmers from Massachusetts struggling to stay out of debtors' prison. "The Tree of Liberty must be refreshed from time to time with the blood of patriots and tyrants," Jefferson wrote then.[6] (This menacing line sometimes appeared on Tea Party paraphernalia, but it was far more popular in the 1990s, among members of that decade's militia movement. On April 19, 1995, the 220th anniversary of the Battle of Lexington and Concord, Timothy McVeigh, who liked to wear a Tree of Liberty T-shirt, blew up the Alfred P. Murrah Federal Building, in Oklahoma City, killing 168 people, including 19 very young children.)[7] But aside from Jefferson, whose enthusiasm for revolution did not survive Robespierre, most everyone else came down in favor of order. "In monarchies the crime of treason or rebellion may admit of being pardoned, or lightly punished," Samuel Adams wrote, during the Shays crisis, "but the man who dares to rebel against the laws of a republic ought to suffer death."[8] James Madison believed America's was a revolution to end all revolutions. And the Constitution, of course, sought "to form a more perfect Union, establish Justice, insure domestic Tranquility, provide for the common defence, promote the general Welfare, and secure the Blessings of Liberty to ourselves and our Posterity." Domestic tranquility was what was called for. The Constitution helped contain the unruliness of the Revolution. So did early accounts of the nation's founding, which tended to emphasize that a revolution had to know when to stop. For the sake of the nation, revolution needed to be a thing of the past.

Meanwhile, though, the Revolution was so brilliant and daring—and, of course, so original and definitive and constitutive—that everyone wanted to claim to have inherited it, especially when running for office or starting a movement or pushing through a piece of legislation. Beginning even before it was over, the Revolution has been put to wildly varying political purposes. Federalists claimed its legacy; so did Anti-Federalists. Supporters of Andrew Jackson's Democratic Party said they were the true sons of the Revolution. No, Whigs said: we are. The Union claimed the Revolution; so, just as fervently, did the Confederacy.[9] In the 1950s, southern segregationists insisted that they were upholding the legacy of the Founding Fathers by adhering to the Constitution. "There is nothing in the United States Constitution that gives the Congress, the President, or the Supreme Court the right to declare that white and colored children must attend the same public schools," said Mississippi senator James Eastland. Advocates of civil rights countered that their movement carried the banner of the Revolution. "Our nation in a sense came into being through a massive act of civil disobedience," Martin Luther King Jr. wrote, "for the Boston Tea Party was nothing but a massive act of civil disobedience." A lot of people talked about the 1964 Civil Rights Act as realizing, at long last, the promise of the Declaration of Independence. Lyndon Johnson compared Selma to Lexington and Concord. The 1965 Voting Rights Act was said to be an end to taxation without representation. "Black people are rebelling in the same way Americans did in the Boston Massacre," Stokely Carmichael said in 1966.[10] That same year, when Johnson signed into law a bill establishing an American Revolution Bicentennial Commission, he used the opportunity to argue for American involvement in Southeast Asia. "Today, the Vietnamese people are fighting for their freedom in South Vietnam. We are carrying forward our great heritage by helping to sustain their efforts."[11] One year later, at the Southern Christian Leadership Conference in Atlanta, King said, "We still need some Paul Revere of conscience to alert every hamlet and every village of America that revolution is still at hand."[12] What all these people meant by "revolution," of course, was different.

"What do We Mean by the Revolution?" Adams asked Jefferson. "The War? That was no part of the revolution. It was only an Effect and Consequence of it. The Revolution was in the Minds of the People, and this was effected from 1760–1775, in the course of fifteen Years, before a drop of blood was shed at Lexington."[13] Adams, like many people, had no doubt that the Revolution had begun in Boston. Oliver thought Massachusetts was "the *Volcano* from whence issued all the Smoak, Flame & Lava, which has since enveloped the whole British american continent."[14] Adams believed the Revolution began in 1760 because, in August of that year, Massachusetts' new, royally appointed governor, Francis Bernard, arrived to find a city in ruins, ravaged, just months before, by the worst fire in any colonial American city, ever. But the city was suffering from worse than fire. Massachusetts had sent more men to fight in the French and Indian War than all of the other colonies combined. Known in Europe as the Seven Years' War, the fighting had started in 1756. Many Massachusetts men had fallen; many more were still to die, buried in unmarked graves, far from home. Boston in 1760 was a city of widows and orphans and wounded soldiers, of struggling artisans and smuggling merchants. Its newspapers were filled with notices of runaway apprentices, of slaves for sale, of bankrupted estates.[15] That December, Boston's James Otis Jr., a thirty-six-year-old lawyer, the most brilliant legal mind of his generation, agreed to take a case arguing against Bernard that the government had acted with arbitrary authority in using an instrument known as writs of assistance to search and seize city merchants' property as part of a campaign against illicit trade.[16] (Otis had another beef with Bernard, who had passed over his father, James Otis Sr., to appoint Thomas Hutchinson as chief of the colony's Superior Court.) The following February, Otis argued the writs of assistance case, which is why Peter Oliver, who also served on the Superior Court, and was Hutchinson's brother-in-law, started his history in 1761. The showdown took place in Boston's Town House (now the Old State House), a three-story Georgian whose east-end gable was topped with gilt statues of the lion and the unicorn, mythical symbols of the British Crown. The Town House sat in the middle of King Street (now State Street), in the heart of the city. The case was heard in the Governor's Council Chamber, on the second floor, a room that boasted an elegant prospect, a wondrous view, straight down the Long Wharf and across the harbor, looking wistfully and a little desperately back to London. John Adams, who was, at the time, an assistant of Otis's law partner, sat among the spectators, in a room tricked out with every trapping of luxury—red velvet–covered mahogany chairs and even ornamented brass spittoons—and of royal authority: Bernard had brought with him full-length portraits of George II and George III to hang alongside the king's arms and a vast map of London.[17] Of Otis's fiery performance that day, Adams later wrote, "American independence was then and there born."[18]

Meanwhile, an ocean away, the *Phillis*, a two-masted, square-rigged ship piloted by Peter Gwin, was cruising the Guinea coast of Africa. After trading English goods for African slaves, Gwin prepared to head to New England. He had sailed to Boston before. He knew how to navigate through the perilous entrance to Boston's harbor, dotted with rocks and shoals and more than thirty islands, tiny and treacherous. Once he got past Castle William, the water would be calmer and the hazards fewer. And then, what beauty, what depths. Wrote one traveler, "within the harbor there is room enough for five hundred sail to lie at an anchor."[19] A sea captain's paradise.

The *Phillis* reached Boston in July of 1761, dropping anchor alongside the Long Wharf, the longest wharf—and the biggest commercial structure—in all of America: 150 feet wide and an audacious 2,000 feet long. On eighteenth-century maps, it looks like a finger pointing across the ocean, pointing home. Gwin's first order of business was to carry his bill of lading the length of the wharf, covered with warehouses and shops, and up the hill to the Customs House, built of rough-hewn stone. To get there, he had to make his way through the dockside bustle of sailors and shipwrights, hawkers and shopkeepers, fishwives and whores, artisans and merchants, the sons and daughters of Europe, Africa, and America. In a city of fifteen thousand people, about a thousand were black, and of that thousand, only eighteen were free.[20] The day Gwin's *Phillis* cleared customs, twenty-two other ships had dropped anchor offshore or tied their leading ropes to the town's fifty-seven wharves. They had sailed from the north: Newfoundland, Quebec; from the south: Connecticut, Rhode Island, New York, Philadelphia, Maryland, Virginia, St. Kitts, Nevis, Bermuda; and from the east, all the way across the wide water: Liverpool and London. Gwin went to the print shop of Benjamin Edes and John Gill, on Queen Street, next door to the town jail, to place an ad in the Boston *Gazette*:

> JUST Imported,
> From *A F R I C A*.
>
> A Number of prime young *S L A V E S*, from the Windward Coast, and to be Sold on board Capt. *Gwin* lying at New-Boston.

This notice caught the eye of a tailor named John Wheatley, who kept a shop on the corner of King Street and Mackerel Lane. Wheatley and his wife, Susanna, took a chaise to the wharf, boarded the ship, and inspected the cargo, men, women, and children brought out of the fetid obscurity below decks to squint against the sun glinting off the water. The girl had lost her two front teeth. That put her at about seven years old. Maybe eight. She was skinny and sick and nearly naked. She was half dead. The captain wanted her off his hands. Wheatley bought her "for a trifle." His wife named her after the ship.[21]

That girl would one day chronicle the birth of the United States:

> Columbia's scenes of glorious toils I write. . . .
> And nations gaze at scenes before unknown![22]

Phillis Wheatley's revolution began in 1761.

The French and Indian War ended in 1763. The imperial coffers were empty: half of Britain's revenues went to paying interest on the war debt. The colonies cost us this war, and the colonists should at least help pay for it, was the logic of George Grenville, the new prime minister. The next year, Parliament passed the Sugar and Currency Acts and warned of a Stamp Act to come. That's why David Ramsay, in his *History*, dated the beginning of the Revolution to 1764. So did Mercy Otis Warren, James Otis's sister, in her three-volume *History of the Rise, Progress, and Termination of the American Revolution*, published in 1805. Mercy Otis, born on Cape Cod in 1728, was three years younger than her brother. Like most girls, she had no formal schooling; instead, she read her brother's books and soaked up his Harvard education. She married James Warren in 1754; they settled in Plymouth. Between 1757 and 1766, she gave birth to five sons. When she wrote her history, she apologized for writing at all—this was man's work—but assured her reader that writing history hadn't hardened her: "The historian has never laid aside the tenderness of the sex."[23]

Warren sited the Revolution's beginning in a room in Boston's Town House just across from the Governor's Council Chamber, Representatives Hall, where her brother, behind the oak speaker's desk, declared taxation without representation to be tyranny. To be governed without consent, to be taxed without representation, Americans liked to argue, "is worse than Death—it is SLAVERY!"[24] This wasn't simply a rhetorical flourish. It was, instead, something between a metaphor and a definition: taxation without representation is slavery.[25] Stephen Hopkins, the governor of Rhode Island, wrote, "those who are governed by the will of another, or of others, and whose property may be taken from them by taxes, or otherwise, without their consent, and against their will, are in the miserable condition of slaves."[26] In *The Rights of the British Colonies Asserted and Proved*, published in 1764, Otis followed the implications of this argument. "Are not women born as free as men? Would it not be infamous to assert that the ladies are all slaves by nature?" And then he argued, at length, on hypocrisy:

> The Colonists are by the law of nature free born, as indeed all men are, white or black. . . . Does it follow that tis right to enslave a man because he is black? Will short curl'd hair like wool . . . help the argument?

No, was Otis's unequivocal answer:

> Nothing better can be said in favor of a trade, that is the most shocking violation of the law of nature, has a direct tendency to diminish the inestimable value of liberty, and makes every dealer in it a tyrant, from the director of an African company to the petty chapman in needles and pins on the unhappy coast. It is a clear truth, that those who every day barter away other men's liberty, will soon care little for their own.[27]

At the time, not everyone could see that as well as Otis did.

Despite colonial opposition to the Sugar and Currency Acts, Parliament passed the Stamp Act the next year, requiring government-issued stamps on pages of printed paper—on, that is, everything from indenture agreements to bills of credit to playing cards. It infuriated many colonists, who were outraged at Parliament's tyrannical reach. "We won't be their negroes," John Adams wrote. The Stamp Act cost lawyers and merchants a few farthings, but it hit printers very hard, requiring them to affix stamps to the pages of their newspapers and to pay stamp collectors a halfpenny for every half sheet—amounting, ordinarily, to a penny for every copy of every issue of every newspaper—and, as if that weren't burden enough, a two shillings' tax on every advertisement. The first cost would drive away subscribers; the second would daunt advertisers. No paper could survive.[28]

Understanding the Stamp Act requires knowing a bit about the history of newspapers. Newspapers date to the sixteenth century; they started as newsletters and newsbooks, copied by hand and sent from one place to another, carrying word of trade and politics. Venetians sold news for a coin called a *gazetta*. Germans read *Zeitungen*; the French perused *nouvelles*; the English paged through intelligencers. The word "newspaper" didn't enter the English language until the 1660s. The *London Gazette* began in 1665. Its news was mostly old, foreign, and unreliable, so unreliable that, in English, the word "gazette" meant, well into the eighteenth century, "rumor-monger." Because early newspapers tended either to arm or to take aim at people in power, they were also sometimes called "paper bullets." In early America, printers were also the editors of the newspapers, and, often, their chief writers. They tended toward irreverence. The first newspaper in the British American colonies, *Publick Occurrences*, was printed in Boston in 1690. It was shut down after just one issue for reporting, among other things, that the king of France had cuckolded his own son. Propping up power is, generally, a less dodgy proposition than defying it. The *Boston News-Letter*, "published by authority"—endorsed by magistrates and ecclesiastics—lasted from 1704 till 1776. In 1719, two more colonial papers began printing: the *Boston Gazette* and, out of Philadelphia, the *American Weekly Mercury*.[29] (Nearly every early American newspaper was issued weekly; it took sixteen hours to set the type for a standard four-page paper.)[30] But James Franklin's *New-England Courant*, launched in 1721, marks the real birth of the American newspaper. It was the first unlicensed paper in the colonies—published without authority—and, while it lasted, it was also, by far, the best. Every other paper looks a rag. The *Courant* contained political essays, opinion, satire, and some word of goings-on. Franklin was the first newspaperman, anywhere in the world, to report the results of a legislative vote count. The *Boston News-Letter* contained, besides the shipping news, tiresome government pronouncements, letters from Europe, and whatever smattering of local news was bland enough to pass the censor. Franklin had a different editorial policy: "I hereby invite all Men, who have Leisure, Inclination and Ability, to speak their Minds with Freedom, Sense and Moderation, and their Pieces shall be welcome to a Place in my Paper."[31]

Franklin was, as a printer, bold unto recklessness. He set as his task the toppling of the Puritan theocracy. He nearly managed it. A fuming Cotton Mather, minister of Boston's Old North Church, dubbed Franklin and his writers the Hell-Fire Club and called his newspaper "A Wickedness never parallel'd any where upon the Face of the Earth!" Undeterred—and, more likely, spurred on—Franklin printed, in the pages of his paper, essay after essay about the freedom of the press. "To anathematize a Printer for publishing the different Opinions of Men," the *Courant* argued, "is as injudicious as it is wicked." For this, and much more, and especially for printing, about Mather, an "Essay against Hypocrites," Franklin was tried for libel, and thrown in jail, twice.[32]

Not long after Franklin started printing the *Courant*, he hired his little brother as an apprentice. In 1721, sixteen-year-old Benjamin Franklin broke upon the literary stage in the guise of a fictional character whose name was a parody of two of Cotton Mather's more dreadful sermons, "Silentiarius" and "Essays to Do Good":

I am courteous and affable, good humour'd (unless I am first provok'd,) and handsome, and sometimes witty, but always, Sir, Your Friend and Humble Servant, SILENCE DOGOOD.

As the sharp-tongued Widow Dogood, the well-drubbed Ben offered "a few gentle Reproofs on those who deserve them," including Harvard students (the colony's ministers-in-training), "Dunces and Blockheads," whose blindness to their good fortune left the poor apprentice all but speechless. Young Franklin then did his caustic widow one better. He invented for her a priggish critic, "Ephraim Censorious," who beseeched Mrs. Dogood to pardon young men their follies and save her scolding for the fair sex, since "Women are prime Causes of a great many Male Enormities."[33] Ahem.

In 1723, a legislative committee charged with investigating James Franklin's *Courant* reported, "The Tendency of the Said paper is to mock Religion, & bring it into Contempt, that the Holy Scriptures are therefore profanely abused, that the Reverend and faithful Ministers of the Gospel are injuriously Reflected on, His Majesty's Government affronted, and the Peace and good Order of his Majesty's Subjects of this Province disturbed."[34] Authorities ordered James Franklin to stop printing the *Courant*. But no one said someone *else* couldn't print it. A notice in the next issue claimed that the paper was "Printed and Sold by BENJAMIN FRANKLIN in Queen Street." As the younger Franklin later fondly recalled, "I had the Management of the Paper, and I made bold to give our Rulers some Rubs in it."[35]

Nevertheless, Benjamin Franklin bridled at working for his brother. He ran away in 1723 and made his way to Philadelphia, where he began printing the *Pennsylvania Gazette*. His brother James died in 1735. By the 1760s, Boston's most spirited printer was a man named Benjamin Edes. In 1755, Edes, the son of a hatter from nearby Charlestown, took over the failing *Boston Gazette* with his lackluster partner, John Gill. Two years later, Boston's selectmen scolded Edes for his impiety: "you have printed Such Pamphlets & such things in your News Papers as reflect grossly upon the received religious principles of this People which is very Offensive. . . . we therefore now Inform you if you go on printing things of this Nature you must Expect no more favours from Us." Edes apologized, promising, in future, to "publish nothing that shall give any uneasiness to any Persons whatever." But he didn't stop. And with the passage of the Stamp Act, the *Boston Gazette* became the organ of the patriot opposition.[36]

In August of 1765, a Boston mob attacked the houses of both the stamp collector, Andrew Oliver (Peter Oliver's brother), and of Thomas Hutchinson, setting loose, fluttering to the winds, the entire manuscript of Hutchinson's *History of Massachusetts*. "Mr. Hutchinson's History contains a valuable collection of facts," wrote Hutchinson's neighbor and close friend, Andrew Eliot, minister of Boston's New North Church, who rescued the pages from gutters and puddles.[37] Beneath an elm forever after known as the Liberty Tree, the crowd hanged Andrew Oliver in effigy and tacked to the effigy a paper purporting to be his confession:

> Fair Freedom's glorious cause I meanly quitted,
> betrayed my country for the sake of pelf,
> But ah! at length the devil hath me outwitted,
> instead of stamping others have hanged my self.

All over the colonies, protesters followed Boston's lead. One observer wrote in the *New York Gazette*, "Our Brethren in

Boston have indeared themselves more than ever to all the colonies in America."[38]

John Singleton Copley, for one, did not find the riots endearing. Copley was born in 1738 in a tobacconist's shop on the Long Wharf. He taught himself to paint, from books, since, by his lights, there was no art in America, but he yearned to see the great galleries of Europe. In September of 1765, he shipped a portrait of his half brother, Henry Pelham, to London, complaining to the ship's captain that the Stamp Act had made "much noise and confusion among us Americans." Copley's portrait, *Boy with a Squirrel*, shows his brother with a pet, tied to a delicate golden chain that dangles over a glass of water, a metaphor for the colonies attachment to the mother country, across the ocean.[39] Copley felt attached.

But that chain was already strained. Edes refused to buy stamps for his newspaper and, at John Adams's suggestion, changed the *Gazette*'s motto to "A free press maintains the majesty of the people."[40] "Working the political Engine," is what Adams called writing for Edes, after a night spent at Edes's shop, "Cooking up Paragraphs" for "the Next Days newspaper."[41] Paul Revere engraved Edes's masthead. In 1765, Edes, Revere, Otis, Hancock, and the Adamses began calling themselves the Sons of Liberty. They met at a place called the Green Dragon Tavern.

The Green Dragon Tavern is also where the twenty-first-century Boston Tea Party held its monthly meetings. A site on Boston's Freedom Trail, just a few steps from Faneuil Hall along the trail's signature red brick path, the Green Dragon billed itself as the "Headquarters of the Revolution." The original building, from 1712, was named after a Green

Dragon Tavern in London.[42] By the front door, a painted statue of a redcoat, the Revolutionary equivalent of a tobacco store Indian, stood guard. The bartender called him Stanley because he stands outside. He brought him in every night. "Quartering the troops," he said.

Christen Varley ran the meeting I went to at the Green Dragon Tavern on March 11, 2010. She was the Boston Tea Party's president. Fierce, cheerful, and determined, Varley, thirty-nine, wore her brown hair in a ponytail, and she was fed up, fed up with the federal government, with taxes and the bailout, with the whole kit and caboodle. "Our topic tonight is that our wonderful federal government is trying to cram health care and whatnot down our throats," she told an audience crowded around a long table in a dimly lit bar that could pass for the set of *Cheers* and where a dozen Tea Partiers sat cheek-by-jowl with almost as many reporters, photographers, television cameramen, and onlookers. Muskets decorated the walls. A Harvard political science graduate student wandered around, trawling for a paper topic. Austin Hess's girlfriend, Kat Malone, was wearing his hat, along with a red, white, and blue T-shirt celebrating the day Scott Brown was elected:

> 1.19.10
> We the People
> HAVE SPOKEN.

Malone, who was from Charlestown, was an avid reader. She'd been working her way through biographies of the Founding Fathers. Beginning in the 1990s, there had been a great glut of these books in the nation's bookstores. They were lively and stirring and, generally, hagiographic; their stories were animated by heroes, larger than life, greater than the greatest generation, an inspiration, better men. Academic historians have criticized biographers for locating the explanation for events in character rather than, say, in larger historical forces, like ideas or politics or culture or economic and social conditions, an approach that has the effect of falsely collapsing the distance between now and then. That's part of the reason why, beginning in the 1960s, many academic historians began writing, instead, about ordinary people, people like artisans, shopkeepers, slaves, and printers.[43] But the charge had also been made that academic historians don't care enough about character or, for that matter, about plot, or storytelling, or writing for anyone other than other academic historians. The family feud between historians and biographers had been going on for long time, without really getting anywhere. (Even Mercy Otis Warren weighed in. For her, history required "a just knowledge of character.")[44] Meanwhile, people like to read books about famous people, the eighteenth-century Harvard-educated elite, like Hancock, the Adamses, Otis, Hutchinson, and the Olivers. Malone had just finished reading a biography of Samuel Adams, and she had found it striking. "It's the same exact issues, all over again," she told me. "They didn't like that the British government was trying to take over their lives."

Doug Bennett, a graduate of Valley Forge Military College who was running for Boston City Council, was at the Green Dragon to court voters. He fumbled in his pockets and handed me a crumpled slip of paper. On it, he had penciled a stanza from Oliver Wendell Holmes's 1873 "Ballad of the Boston Tea-Party," which he recited, with feeling:

No! Ne'er was mingled such a draught
In palace, hall, or arbor,

As freeman brewed and tyrants quaffed,
That night in Boston Harbor![45]

I sat down next to George Egan, a soft-spoken Boston cop, retired and living on a pension. He told me he'd been a Democrat until "Kennedy killed that little girl" (1969, Teddy, Mary Jo Kopechne, Chappaquiddick) and had never worked on a political campaign until Brown's, but then he threw himself into it because "the government is out of control." Around the table, everyone was gabby and excited. There was much talk of voter guides, primaries, and the November elections and, in the nearer term, an activist training session run by the American Majority, where, Varley said, "we will learn how to be conservative activists and learn to do what the other people have been doing for the last forty years." She had an important announcement: the Tea Party Express would be bringing the former governor of Alaska and John McCain's erstwhile running mate, Sarah Palin, to Massachusetts on April 14, for a rally on the Boston Common, the day before the Tax Day protest on the Washington Mall. (The Tea Party Express was funded by a political action committee called Our Country Deserves Better, which was launched during the 2008 election, when it sponsored a "Stop Obama" bus tour.) Palin's visit, Varley said, was good news, "no matter what you think of her." She talked about the game plan for the big day: "The Obama Hitler sign. Let's look out for those people, and make sure people know, they're not us." Someone ventured that the problem was that too few people know that the "tea" in Tea Party is an acronym. Blank stares, all around. "Taxed Enough Already. People need to know that's what we stand for."

Edward Wagner, a middle-aged Republican from Jamaica Plain, agreed. "We need to disabuse the public of some of the more exotic rumors out there." Like everyone I met at the Green Dragon, Wagner was chatty, but he didn't trust the press or, at least, he didn't trust what the far right called the "lamestream media," including the *Boston Globe.* "I saw people's eyes start out of their heads on the twentieth," Wagner said, talking about the day Brown was elected, "because they had read the *Globe* poll, and the funny thing is, they believed it, they believed the liberal media." Austin Hess later told me, "I don't read books; I read blogs." I once asked Hess what he thought of Glenn Beck. (A 2010 New York Times / CBS News poll reported that "63 percent of self-described Tea Party supporters gain most of their television news from Fox, compared with 23 percent of all adult Americans.")[46] "He's given to hyperbole and he's a bit emotional," Hess said, "but, substantively, I haven't yet found anything I disagree with him about." Patrick Humphries, a software engineer from Bedford, a town out past Lexington, told me on another night that he got much of his news from the Drudge Report, which he read every day at lunch. "The media is filtered in this country," Humphries said, but "the new media has made it so the old media can't get away with it anymore." The old media wasn't just old. It was dying.

"It will affect Printers more than anybody," Benjamin Franklin warned Parliament about the Stamp Act, a piece of legislation that turned out to be Britain's first and arguably its worst mistake in trying to manage the American colonies ("Grenville's greatest blunder," Arthur Schlesinger Sr. once called it).[47] Printers, more than anybody, better than anybody, could fight back. When Massachusetts' governor, Francis Bernard, who believed that Benjamin Edes's *Boston Gazette* "swarmed with Libells of the most atrocious kind," threatened Edes

and Gill with prosecution, John Adams urged the printers
on. Do not, he told them, "suffer yourselves to be wheedled
out of your liberty by any pretences of politeness, delicacy, or
decency. These, as they are often used, are but three names
for hypocrisy, chicanery, and cowardice." Tories took to calling the *Gazette* the "Weekly Dung Barge."[48] Edes, though,
wasn't easily wheedled out of anything. Ramsay, in his *History*, wrote, "It was fortunate for the liberties of America,
that News-papers were the subject of a heavy stamp duty.
Printers, when uninfluenced by government, have generally
arranged themselves on the side of liberty, nor are they less
remarkable for attention to the profits of their profession."[49]

The Stamp Act—the "fatal *Black-Act*," one printer called
it—was set to go into effect on November 1, 1765.[50] In October, colonists convened a Stamp Act Congress in New York,
where delegates drafted and signed a declaration, asserting,
above all, "that it is inseparably essential to the Freedom of
a People, and the undoubted Right of *Englishmen*, that no
Taxes be imposed on them but with their own consent, given
personally, or by their Representatives."[51] On October 10,
1765, a Baltimore printer changed his newspaper's title to the
Maryland Gazette, Expiring. Its dread motto: "In Uncertain
Hopes of a Resurrection to Life Again." Later that month,
the printer of the *Pennsylvania Journal* replaced his newspaper's masthead with a death's head and framed his front
page with a thick black border in the shape of a gravestone.
"Adieu, Adieu!" whispered the ghastly *Journal*. On October
31, the *New-Hampshire Gazette* appeared with black mourning borders and, in a column on the front page, lamented its
own demise, groaning, "I must *Die!*" Shrieked the *Connecticut Courant*, quoting the book of Samuel: "Tell it not in Gath!
Publish it not in Askalon!"[52] The newspaper is dead!

Or, not quite dead yet. "Before I make my *Exit*," gasped the *New-Hampshire Gazette*, "I will recount over the many good Deeds I have done, and how useful I have been, and still may be, provided my Life should be spar'd; or I might hereafter revive again." The list of deeds was long and wonderful; it ran to four columns. Nothing good in the world had ever happened but that a printer set it in type. "Without this Art of communicating to the Public, how dull and melancholy must all the intelligent Part of Mankind appear?" It's a fair question, before and since. But besides the settling over the land of a pall of melancholy and dullness, what else happens when a newspaper dies? In one allegory published during the Stamp Act crisis, a tearful *Liberty* cried to her dying brother, *Gazette*, "Unless thou revivest quickly, I shall also perish with thee! In our Lives we were not divided; in our Deaths we shall not be separated!"[53]

The day the Stamp Act went into effect, Edes draped his *Gazette* in black mourning ink and Bostonians staged a Funeral for Liberty, burying a coffin six feet under the Liberty Tree. In his paper, Edes reported on similar funerals held all over the colonies. Everywhere, the story ended the same way. In Portsmouth, New Hampshire, "a coffin was prepared, and neatly ornamented, on the lid of which was inscribed the word *Liberty*, in capitals, aged one hundred and forty-five years, computing the time of our ancestors landing at Plymouth." But then, lo, a reprieve, otherworldly: the eulogy "was scarcely ended before the corpse was taken up, it having been perceived that some remains of life were left."[54]

The old media, or what Edward Wagner called the "liberal media," used to be known as the mainstream media, and its notions of fairness date to the eighteenth century. The elusive pursuit of journalistic objectivity only began in the nineteenth century, but the best eighteenth-century printers had standards, too.[55] "The Business of Printing has chiefly to do with Men's Opinions," Benjamin Franklin wrote, in "An Apology for Printers," in 1731. Printers were bound to offend, Franklin explained, but his conscience was clear so long as he published a sufficient range of opinion: "Printers are educated in the Belief, that when Men differ in Opinion, both Sides ought equally to have the Advantage of being heard by the Publick; and that when Truth and Error have fair Play, the former is always an overmatch for the latter."[56]

In 2009, while the Tea Party was forming, the newspaper was dying, all over again. This was more than a coincidence; it was a cause. The decline of the newspaper had destabilized American politics. A website called the Newspaper Death Watch kept count, with a column titled "R.I.P." One hundred and forty-five newspapers either stopped publishing a print edition or shut down entirely that year. Nearly six hundred newspapers laid off employees. On an average day in 2009, forty newspaper employees lost their jobs.[57] And this time around, there was no sign of a reprieve.

"These meetings are just fun because we do everything else by e-mail," Christen Varley told me. Varley entered politics by way of the blogosphere. "I'm from Ohio," she said. "Massachusetts is a foreign country to me." She moved to Massachusetts in 2004, for her husband's job, and, although, with the exception of an internship with the Ohio Republican Party in 1992, she'd never been involved in politics before, living in Taxachusetts triggered something in her. "I started blogging in 2006, and in early 2009 I just thought we should have a Tax Day thing." Varley's old blog is called GOPMom: "Mom Knows Best!" She organized Boston's three Tea Party rallies in 2009: Tax Day, the Fourth of July, and 9/12. Her concerns included "the myth of anthropogenic global warming."

Global warming she believed to be a conspiracy of the liberal media. She had been home raising her daughter, but in 2009 she took a job with the Coalition for Marriage and Family, a nonprofit formed to try to get a ban on same-sex marriage on the ballot. Its motto was "One Man, One Woman." I asked her whether that didn't amount to more government interference, but the problem, she said, was that the government had interfered so much already that it had nearly destroyed the family, and the only thing for it was to use the government to repair the damage.

All evening, people came and went and milled about. Varley stayed put. Behind her hung a huge framed print, depicting a group of patriots, drinking in this very tavern—something, stylistically, between a Currier and Ives engraving and the label on Sam Adams beer. That beer label happens to have been drawn by Jean Paul Tibbels, illustrator of the American Girl doll books. You'd figure the guy on Sam Adams beer must be Adams, who was, briefly, a brewer, but it's not. It's a cartoon of a portrait of Paul Revere, painted by Copley in 1768. Copley painted Revere, a silversmith, in a waistcoat and shirtsleeves, sitting at his bench, working. A couple of years later, he painted Adams, too, but as a bewigged and learned gentleman, in a buttoned frock, standing at a desk strewn with papers, not the sort of man to sell beer.

Varley was sitting, perfectly centered, in front of and just below that picture of the Sons of Liberty, which made it seem as if they were anointing her. That's what had drawn all those photographers and television crews. I asked her what it meant to her that patriots had plotted here. "We admire their battle," she said. "But we're not melting down horseshoes for musket balls."

CHAPTER 2

The Book of Ages

WHEREIN WILL BE FOUND AN ACCOUNT OF AN
EXTRAORDINARY ASSEMBLY—A DISPUTE BETWEEN
MR. ADAMS AND MRS. WARREN—THE SUFFERINGS OF
ANOTHER LADY—POOR RICHARD'S WAY TO WEALTH—A
LATE MASSACRE IN BOSTON—ANOTHER ILL-CONSIDERED
INVASION—A PLEA FOR PEACE—AND REFLECTIONS ON THE
FALLACY OF PRESENTISM

On March 20, 2010, the day before the U.S. House of Representatives was scheduled to vote on the health care bill, the Boston Tea Party held an Anti-Obamacare rally in front of Faneuil Hall. A few dozen people turned up. Most carried signs: "The Constitution SPEAKS." Some waved flags of thirteen stars. Acolytes of Ayn Rand urged, "READ ATLAS SHRUGGED." Christen Varley told a woman who showed up with a Hitler sign to leave. The place was bustling with tourists on their way to shop at Quincy Market. Austin Hess, wearing his tricorn and a mock–Obama campaign T-shirt that read NOPE instead of HOPE, summed up his objectives for the Tea Party movement: "I want to replace the current political establishment, get all incumbents out and replace them with fiscal conservatives who will abide by the Constitution."

Hess had moved to Massachusetts from Virginia three years before. "We're trying to get back to what the founders had," he told me. "We're trying to bring people back to Boston's roots. Liberty above all." A nurse from Worcester who grew up in the Midwest and was registered as an Independent explained what getting back to those eighteenth-century roots meant to her: "I don't want the government giving money to people who don't want to work. Government is for the post office, and to defend our country, and maybe for the roads. That's all."

"The history of our revolution will be one continued lye from one end to the other," Johns Adams once predicted.[1] He was right to worry. In every nation, as in every family, some stories are remembered, others are forgotten, and there are always some stories too painful to tell. Adams expected that the Revolution, a messy, sprawling, decades-long affair, would, over time, be shortened and simplified. In the national imagination, the Revolution is a fable. Much of what most people picture when they think about the Revolution comes from the world of juvenilia—*Johnny Tremain*, paper dolls, elementary school art projects, and family vacations—which isn't surprising, and wouldn't be a problem, except that every history of a nation's founding makes an argument about the nature of its government.

People would make of the Revolution what they needed, Adams knew, and what they needed would rarely agree with how he saw it, or what he thought mattered. Adams was especially worried that the nation's story of its origins might one day leave him out altogether. (Adams had worried that history would neglect him even before he accomplished anything of which anyone might take any note. One night in 1759, when he was twenty-four and just starting out, he woke up, seized with an aching void in his chest. He picked up his quill, reached for his inkpot, and wrote in his diary, "I feel anxious, eager, after something. What is it?" It was the same thing it always was: the pain of his insatiable ambition. "I have a dread of Contempt, a quick sense of Neglect, a strong Desire of Distinction," Adams wrote that night.)[2] In 1807, when Adams read Mercy Otis Warren's *History*, twelve hundred pages in three volumes that devoted a scant four pages to one John Adams, his worst fears were realized. Sputtering with rage, Adams wrote Warren ten letters—some more than twenty pages long—of petty, rambling vituperation. Warren had assailed his character: "In the 392d page of the third volume, you say that 'Mr. Adams, his passions and prejudices were sometimes too strong for his sagacity and judgment.'" She had neglected him: "You have carefully recorded the appointment of Mr. Jay to Madrid, in page 141, Vol. II, to have been on the 27th of September, 1779, yet have taken no notice of mine, which was on the 29th of the same month." She would not even grant him alphabetic preeminence. When Warren listed Franklin, Jay, and Adams as ambassadors, Adams complained that his name ought to have appeared first in that list, as it had in their commission. "You will say, no doubt, that this is 'sighing for rank,'" he sneered, anticipating her objection. "Very well: say so, Mrs. Warren. Make the most of it."

Against Adams's abuse, Warren fought back. "Were she to write her History over again, and correct her *errors*, as you seem to wish her to do," she answered, what must she write? "She must tell the world that Mr. Adams . . . had neither ambition nor pride of talents . . . ; that his writings suppressed rebellion, quelled the insurgents, established the State and Federal Constitutions, and gave the United States all the liberty, republicanism, and independence they enjoy; that his name was always placed at the head of every public commission; that nothing had been done, and nothing could be done, neither in Europe nor America, without his sketching and drafting the business, from the first opposition to British measures in the year 1764 to signing the treaty of peace with England in the year 1783." Who would believe such rot? "Mr. Adams might indeed think this a very pleasant portrait, but I doubt whether the world would receive it as a better likeness than the one drawn" in her own history.[3] Ah, but give it time, Mrs. Warren.

In 2008, Adams was the subject of an Emmy Award–winning HBO miniseries, based on David McCullough's Pulitzer Prize–winning biography. Independence was almost entirely Adams's doing, HBO suggested, despite the fact that, to the American people, Thomas Paine was the most important promoter of independence; Adams's crucial and, by all accounts, dazzling and stirring speech before the Second Continental Congress, urging independence, does not survive; and Adams didn't write the document declaring it. ("I am obnoxious, suspected, and unpopular," Adams told Jefferson, graciously offering the task of drafting the Declaration of Independence to the Virginian. He forever regretted this. "Jefferson ran away with all the stage effect," Adams later complained, "and all the glory.")[4] None of this gave HBO pause: its Franklin was a buffoon, its Washington a sap-skull, its Jefferson distracted and, finally, deluded. Thomas Paine didn't even have a part. HBO's *John Adams* was animated as much by the man's many private resentments as by the birth of the United States. It was history, with a grudge. "He United the States of America" was the miniseries' motto, giving credit to Adams for . . . everything.[5]

The history of the Revolution hasn't been one continued lie from one end to the other, as Adams would have it, but it's certainly been changeable, as, in fact, it ought. History is an endlessly interesting argument where evidence is everything and storytelling is everything else. That John Adams and Mercy Otis Warren didn't see eye to eye on Adams's contribution to American independence might not seem of any great consequence, but it's a good illustration of how two people—even two people who lived through it—can read the same evidence differently. The telling of history is, by its very nature, controversial, contentious, and contested; it advances by debate. This doesn't make history squishy, vague, and irrelevant. It makes it picky, demanding, and vital. American history, though, is beset by this paradox: historical analysis is unstable because, like all scholarship, it must be forever subject to interpretation and revision and, especially, to new evidence, new vantage points, and new avenues of investigation, but history plays a civic role too, and a nation born in revolution looks for stability, tranquility, and permanence, even in its own past. And, because of the nature of the Constitution, the founding bears a particular burden: it is a story about what binds Americans together—We the people, do ordain—but it also serves as the final source of political authority, the ultimate arbiter of every argument, the last court of appeal. No history can easily or always bear that weight.

"History is not the Province of the Ladies," John Adams concluded, after reading Warren's *History*.[6] In the eighteenth century, even writing wasn't the province of women. "The confusion & distres those Opresive Actts have thrown us Poor Americans into is un Discribable by me," Benjamin Franklin's sister, Jane Mecom, wrote to him from Boston, the month after the Stamp Act went into effect. Mecom could read—"I read as much as I Dare," she once wrote to her brother—and she could write, if not well. "I have such a Poor Fackulty at making Leters," she apologized. Franklin would have none of it; he knew his sister's pride well enough not to credit her humility. "Is there not a little Affectation in your Apology for the Incorrectness of your Writing?" he teased her. "Perhaps it is rather fishing for Commendation. You write better, in my Opinion, than most American Women."[7] He was, sadly, right.

Born in 1712, Jane Franklin was the youngest of seven daughters; Benjamin, born in 1706, was the youngest of ten sons. Jenny and Benny, they were called when they were little. Their father was a candle-maker and soap-boiler. One of the Franklin children drowned in a tub of suds, at the age of three, when everyone was so busy making soap and dipping candles that no one saw him fall in. Jenny and Benny had very different childhoods. In early America, boys learned to read and write; girls were taught to read and stitch. Boys held quills; girls held needles.

> I am obnoxious to each carping tongue
> Who says my hand a needle better fits

wrote the Puritan poet Anne Bradstreet. In 1710, only two in every five women in New England could sign their names, and most could do no more writing than that. (To sign your name is one thing; to write prose is quite another.) Massachusetts Poor Laws required masters of apprentices to teach "males to write, females to read." In 1744, a poem in the *Boston Evening Post* had a husband saying to his wife, concerning the education of their daughter,

> Teach her what's useful, how to shun deluding
> To roast, to toast, to boil and mix a pudding

> To knit, to spin, to sew, to make or mend,
> To scrub, to rub, to earn and not to spend.

Teaching girls to write was frivolous. Even teaching them to read could be dangerous: it might make them poor wives. "My wife does hardly one earthly thing but read, read, read, almost from the time she gets up, to the time she goes to bed," wrote an essayist in the *American Magazine* in 1769. "I hope all unmarried tradesmen, when they have read this letter, will take special care how they venture upon a bookish woman."[8]

After her brother Benjamin ran away from home, Jane Franklin married her next-door neighbor, Edward Mecom, a saddler. She was fifteen; he was twenty-seven. Unlike her brother, she never wrote an autobiography, but she did keep a tiny, fourteen-page notebook she called her "Book of Ages." In it, she recorded the births and deaths of her children. It begins,

> Josiah Mecom their first Born on Wednesday June the 4: 1729 and Died May the 18-1730.[9]

Josiah Mecom died before his first birthday. Jane Mecom gave birth eleven times more. All but one of her children died before she did.

She also struggled, desperately, to stay out of the places you could go, in eighteenth-century Boston, if you didn't have any money: debtors' prison, the Manufactory House (a workhouse), and an almshouse run by the Overseers of the Poor. In 1763, 1764, and twice in 1765, the sheriff of Boston came to Jane Mecom's house, looking for her husband and threatening to take him to debtors' prison. But before the sheriff could catch him, Edward Mecom died. "Nothing but troble can you hear from me," Jane Mecom wrote in September of 1765. "It Pleased God to Call my Husband out of this Troblesom world where he had Injoyed Litle & suffered much by Sin & Sorrow." In December, while Franklin was in London, answering parliamentary inquiries about the Stamp Act, his sister wrote to him: "my Income suplys us with vitles fiering candles & Rent but more it cannot with all the Prudence I am mistres of, but thus I must Rub along till Spring when I must strive after some other way but what at Present I cant tell." Edward Mecom left his wife with nothing but debts, not least because, long before he died, he had lost his mind. Whatever ailed him, it was heritable. When Jane's son Peter fell prey to the Mecom madness, Benjamin Franklin paid a farmer's wife to take care of him.[10]

Whenever I hear people like that nurse from Worcester talk about getting back to what the founders had, which she believes to be a government that won't give money to people who don't work, I think about Peter Franklin Mecom: he was tied up in a barn, like an animal, for the rest of his life. I don't want to go back to that.

Benjamin Franklin had hopes for another of his nephews, his namesake, to become a printer. "The way to wealth, if you desire it, is plain as the way to market," Franklin wrote, in "Advice to a Young Tradesman from an Old One": "It depends chiefly on two words, *industry* and *frugality*."[11] I think Franklin wrote that advice for Benjamin Mecom. He placed him in an apprenticeship in New York. "I have a very good opinion of Benny in the main," Franklin wrote his sister, "and have great hopes of his becoming a worthy man, his faults being only such as are commonly incident to boys of his years, and he has many good qualities, for which I love him."[12] In New York, the young apprentice proved ungovernable. Franklin next arranged for him to take over a printing business in Antigua. Still, he was worried. "In my opinion, if Benny can but be prevailed on to behave steadily, he may make his fortune there," he wrote Jane, but "without some share of steadiness and perseverance, he can succeed no where."[13] In sending his nephew to Antigua, Franklin made the same arrangement that he had made with other junior partners: Franklin supplied the printing house and the types in exchange for one-third of the profits. But when Jane Mecom moved to a house on Hanover Street, in Boston's North End, Franklin proposed different terms: Benjamin Mecom need pay his uncle no more than a small amount of sugar and rum, so long as he would pay his mother's rent.[14] Unfortunately, in Antigua, Mecom printed little and sold less. It wasn't long before Franklin began warning a bookseller in London not to front him too much inventory. "Pray keep him within Bounds," Franklin cautioned, "and do not suffer him to be more than Fifty Pounds in your Debt." He had by now begun to apologize for his errant nephew: "He is a young Lad, quite unacquainted with the World."[15]

Mecom failed in Antigua, and returned to New York. But Franklin didn't abandon him. In 1757, when Franklin was stuck in New York, waiting to sail to England, he furnished his nephew, Benjamin Mecom, with a horse, to ride to Boston, where Franklin had established for him another printing shop. In New York, Franklin also wrote his sister three letters. And he wrote a new will, leaving to her both the mortgage on a house in Boston, and his share of their father's estate.[16] Finally, he wrote an essay that came to be called "The Way to Wealth." The reason Rick Santelli thinks Benjamin Franklin would be rolling over in his grave over Americans paying their neighbor's mortgages is because "The Way to Wealth," Franklin's most famous essay, has been read as if Franklin were the Founding Father of free enterprise. But "The Way to Wealth" was, among other things, a set of rules Franklin was giving to his poor, profligate, and unsteady nephew. And it was also something of a parody of just that kind of advice as, finally, not worth much.

Franklin, who had launched his literary career as Mrs. Silence Dogood, loved pseudonyms, satires, and shams of every sort. Beginning in 1732, he had been printing *Poor Richard's Almanack*, using the pseudonym Richard Saunders. (The word *poor* in the title of an almanac was an eighteenth-century term of art, a promise that a book would be funny and a warning that it might be vulgar. Poor Richard's rivals included Poor Robin and Poor Will.) Almanacs forecast twelve months' worth of weather; Franklin knew this for nonsense: in 1741, Poor Richard predicted only sunshine, explaining to his Courteous Reader, "To oblige thee the more, I have omitted all the bad Weather, being Thy Friend R.S."[17]

Franklin wrote all sorts of lampoons. He once wrote a parody of a gentleman's conduct manual, a letter advising a young man suffering from "that hard-to-be-govern'd Passion of Youth," but unwilling to seek marriage as a remedy for what ailed him, to take only older women for mistresses because they're wiser, better talkers, better at intrigue, and better at other things, too, "every Knack being by Practice capable of Improvement"; not to mention, "They are *so* grateful!!" Another time, he wrote a fake chapter of the Old Testament, a parable attacking religious persecution, in pitch-perfect King James, and had it printed and bound within the pages of his own Bible so that he could read it aloud, to see who would fall for it.[18]

Franklin wrote "The Way to Wealth" in the voice of Richard Saunders; he told a story. He had recently stopped his horse at an auction, where one Father Abraham, "a plain clean old Man, with white Locks," stood before a crowd. *"Pray, Father Abraham, what think you of the Times?"* the crowd asked the old man. *"Won't these heavy Taxes quite ruin the Country? How shall we be ever able to pay them?"* Father Abraham then answered with a speech strung together from more than ninety of Poor Richard's proverbs, endorsing thrift and hard work, including "Early to Bed, and early to rise, makes a Man healthy, wealthy and wise."[19] The speech's proverbs, though, were no fair sample of Poor Richard's wisdom, which was not mostly or even very much about money and how to get it. If Franklin hadn't been so worried about taxes, or about his wayward nephew, he might instead have pulled together some of Poor Richard's many proverbs about equality: "The greatest monarch on the proudest throne, is oblig'd to sit upon his own arse." Or hypocrisy: "He that is conscious of a Stink in his Breeches, is jealous of every Wrinkle in another's Nose." Or religion: "Serving God is Doing good to Man, but Praying is thought an easier Service, and therefore more generally chosen." Or, he might have chosen to collect the dozens of Poor Richard's proverbs advising *against* the accumulation of wealth: "The Poor have little, Beggars none; the Rich too much, enough not one."[20] Instead, Franklin chose proverbs advising thrift. And then he sent a copy to Benjamin Mecom, in Boston, who, as Franklin must have urged him, issued Franklin's essay as a pamphlet, becoming the first of very many printers to do so. "The Way to Wealth" was reprinted in at least 145 editions and six languages even before the eighteenth century was over.[21] But Benjamin Mecom couldn't print his way to wealth. Nothing could save him. By now, he was acting so strangely, setting type in his best dress—coat, wig, hat, gloves, and ruffles—that Boston's printers gave him the nickname Queer Notions.[22] Benjamin Mecom was going mad.

In 1766, Parliament repealed the Stamp Act. When news of the repeal reached Boston, the city was lit up with candles, an obelisk was erected in the Common, and fireworks were set off. The spirit of liberty was in the air. The next week, Boston's Town Meeting, following Worcester's, voted to instruct its members "for the total abolishing of slavery from among us; that you move for a law, to prohibit the importation and purchasing of slaves for the future."[23] In Cambridge, students thumbed their noses at their tutors. Undergraduates calling themselves the Sons of Harvard walked out of Commons, protesting rancid butter and declaring, in the words of Asa Dunbar (Henry David Thoreau's grandfather), "Behold our Butter stinketh!"[24] Boston merchant Nathaniel Appleton hoped to honor the Stamp Act struggle otherwise. In *Considerations on Slavery*, printed by Edes and Gill, he urged the passage of an antislavery bill, arguing that it would be a fitting memorial. "The years 1765 & 1766 will be ever memorable for the glorious stand which America has made for her Liberties; how much glory will it add to us if at the same time we are establishing Liberty for ourselves and children, we show the same regard to all mankind that came among us?"[25] Appleton thought the time had come to end slavery. He was off by a century.

In 1767, Parliament levied the Townshend Duties, taxes on tea, paper, and other goods. "Sorrows roll upon me like the waves of the sea," Mecom wrote to her brother that year. She recorded another death in her Book of Ages: "Died my

Dear & Beloved Daughter Polly Mecom." In her grief, she despaired:

> The Lord giveth and the Lord taketh away oh may I never be so Rebelious as to Refuse Acquesing & & saying from my hart Blessed be the Name of the Lord.

And then she put down her pen. Those were the last words she ever wrote in her Book of Ages. God knows, there were more deaths, but she left them unchronicled.[26]

Bostonians set about boycotting British imports and spurning luxury of every sort just when Jane Mecom, who had also taken in boarders, was trying to rub along by making fancy bonnets to sell to merchants' wives. "It Proves a Litle unlucky for me," she wrote to her brother, "that our People have taken it in there Heads to be so Exsesive Frugal at this Time as you will see by the Newspapers our Blusterers must keep themselves Imployed & If they Do no wors than Perswade us to were our old cloaths over again I cant Disaprove of that in my Hart tho I should Like to have those that do bye & can afford it should bye what Litle I have to sell." Boycotting was all well and good, but it hit the poor hardest. By now, Benjamin Mecom was in debtors' prison in Philadelphia.[27]

Boycotting Bostonians proved so forbiddingly unwilling to pay the Townshend Duties and Governor Bernard so hapless at restraining their protests that the British Army arrived, to maintain order. In October of 1768, a month after Boston's merchants signed a formal agreement to boycott British goods, two regiments of regular infantry wearing coats the color of boiled lobster disembarked from ships in the harbor, marched through the streets of the city, wheeling massive artillery, and pitched camp in Boston Common. Bernard gave the officers the keys to the Town House. Another regiment of soldiers laid siege to the Manufactory House, availing themselves of a Quartering Act passed by Parliament in 1764. Andrew Eliot despaired, "Good God! What can be worse to a people who have tasted the sweets of liberty!"[28]

Four days after the redcoats landed, someone stole into Harvard Hall, in Cambridge, took a knife to a three-quarterlength portrait of Bernard, painted by Copley, and cut from the canvas the shape of a heart. The culprit left behind a note explaining that this "was a most charitable attempt to deprive him of that part, which a retrospect upon his administration must have rendered exquisitely painful." Bernard: you heartless bastard. Copley attempted a repair. "Our American limner, Mr. Copley, by the surprising art of his pencil, has actually restored as *good a heart* as had been taken from it," Edes reported, "tho' upon a near and accurate inspection, it will be found to be no other than *a false one.*—There may it long remain *hanging*, to shew posterity the true picture of the man, who during a weak and wicked Administration, was suffered to continue in the seat of Government, a sore scourge to the people, until he had happily awakened a whole continent to a thorough sense of their own interest, and thereby laid the foundation of American greatness."[29] Before the year was out, Bernard was recalled to London, and Thomas Hutchinson was named acting governor. Copley who, in 1767, had married the daughter of a prominent Tory merchant, contemplated a crossing, too. "You have nothing to Hazard in Comeing to this Place," Benjamin West wrote to him from London.[30]

"The whol conversation of this Place turns upon Politics," Jane Mecom wrote to her brother, "as you will see by the News Papers If you give yr self the Troble to Read them, But they will not Infalably Informe you of the Truth; for Every thing that any Designing Person has a mind to Propagate Is stufed into them." Jane Mecom came from a family of printers, but she didn't have much use for blusterers: "for my Part I wish we had Let alone strife before it was medled with & folowed things that make for Peace."[31]

The arrival of the army, far from containing the crisis, exploded it. Paul Revere made an engraving, titled *The Landing of the British Troops in Boston*, and Phillis Wheatley, who, now about fifteen years old, had begun writing poetry, juvenilia, composed a verse: "On the Arrival of the Ships of War, and the Landing of the Troops." (It does not survive.)[32] The British placed two cannons at the base of the Town House, facing, not toward the Long Wharf and across the ocean at invading enemies, but into the town. The legislature moved to Cambridge, to meet in Harvard Hall. Edes began preparing a daily *Journal of the Times*, stories, most written by Samuel Adams and not all of them true, about atrocities committed by redcoats on the people of Boston, like the one about a woman, raped by a soldier, who staggered across the Common only to die beneath the Liberty Tree. Picked up and printed in newspapers across the colonies, the syndicated *Journal of the Times* proved crucial to the resistance movement (and has been credited with originating the political exposé as a journalistic form). Attempting to rouse support in the southern colonies, Edes's writers also charged British officers in Boston with attempting to incite a slave rebellion by trying "to persuade some Negro servants to ill-treat and abuse their masters, assuring them that the soldiers were come to procure their freedoms, and that with their help and assistance they should be able to drive all the Liberty Boys to the devil."[33]

The specter of slave rebellion wielded massive political power in the eighteenth century. Everywhere in the colonies, slaves who murdered their owners were subject to the most atrocious punishments meted out in the English-speaking world. In Antigua, in 1736, some black men convicted of conspiracy were roasted alive, others were broken on the wheel, and some starved to death. Five years later, thirteen black men were burned at the stake in New York City, and seventeen more were hanged, for conspiring to burn the city down and murder their masters. In 1755, a black woman convicted of poisoning her owner, a merchant from Charlestown, was burned at the stake in Cambridge; her coconspirator, a man named Mark, was hanged in an iron gibbet on Boston Neck.[34] Some Sons of Liberty, like Otis and Appleton, might argue for an end to slavery, but New England was by no means seized with abolitionist fervor; slave owners in Massachusetts, as everywhere, lived in fear of insurrection. In 1769, a British captain stationed in Boston was indicted by a grand jury "for stirring up, exciting, and encouraging the Negro slaves in Boston to a conspiracy against their masters."[35]

The people of Boston were offended by the British Army: the soldiers swore; they were rapists, papists, blasphemers, infidels, Irish; they were inciting a slave rebellion. "The town is now a perfect garrison," Edes's *Journal* reported.

> What an appearance does Boston now make! One of the first commercial towns in America, has now several regiments of soldiers quartered in the midst of it, and even the Merchants Exchange is picquetted, and made the spot where the main guard is placed and paraded, and their cannon mounted; so that instead of our merchants and trading people transacting

their business, we see it filled with red coats, and have our ears dinn'd with the music of the drum and fife.[36]

In September of 1769, a British customs commissioner beat James Otis on the head, badly, with a cane. Even before the beating, Otis had been unstable. "His imagination flames, his passions blaze," John Adams had written in his diary. "He is liable to great inequalities of temper." Now he grew worse. "Mr. Speaker, the liberty of this country is gone forever! and I'll go after it!" Otis hollered from the floor of the Assembly, and then ran out the door. "He rambles and wanders like a ship without a helm," Adams wrote.[37] Otis ran through the streets of Boston, naked, firing a musket and smashing windows, helter-skelter.[38] Watching her brother's decline, Mercy Otis Warren prayed for her own sanity:

> From reason's laws let me ne'er swerve
> But calmly, mistress of my mind.[39]

Otis was declared incompetent, and carried, like Peter Franklin Mecom, to the countryside, bound hand and foot.[40]

"A series of occurrences," the Boston Town Meeting declared in early 1770, "afford great reason to believe that a deep-laid and desperate plan of imperial despotism has been laid, and partly executed, for the extinction of all civil liberty." That their king had ordered British soldiers to take up arms against them only further fueled Bostonians' fears that their liberties were being destroyed, one by one. In decrying the king's army, Bostonians were much influenced by John Trenchard's treatise, *An Argument, Shewing, that a Standing Army Is Inconsistent with a Free Government.* Trenchard wrote, "If we look through the World, we shall find in no Country, Liberty and an Army stand together;

to know whether a People are Free or Slaves, it is necessary only to ask, whether there is an Army kept amongst them." Some colonists began to suspect a vast conspiracy. Jefferson would look back at the years between 1765 and 1770 and agree that while "single acts of tyranny may be ascribed to the accidental opinion of a day, a series of oppressions . . . too plainly prove a deliberate and systematical plan of reducing us to slavery." For many in the colonies, both inside and outside Boston, the arrival of the army offered the best proof, the final proof they needed, of just such a plot. "The MONSTER of a standing ARMY," one colonist wrote, was borne of "a PLAN . . . systematically laid, and pursued by the British ministry . . . for enslaving America."[41]

When the troops landed, Andrew Eliot offered a grim prediction: "there will never be that harmony between Great Britain and her colonies than there hath been; all confidence is at an end; and the moment there is any blood shed all affection will cease."[42] That moment came. "Not the battle of Lexington or Bunker Hill, not the surrender of Burgoyne or Cornwallis," John Adams would later write, "were more important events in American history than the battle of King street on the 5th of March, 1770."[43]

About nine o'clock on March 5, 1770, the bells in Boston's churches rang out the alarm for fire. From across the city, men and boys raced to the Town House, carrying leather fire buckets and crying, "Fire, fire!" "There is no fire," young Benjamin Davis told a ropemaker named Samuel Gray. "It is the soldiers fighting." Gray kept on running to King Street, shouting over his shoulder, "Damn their bloods." Thomas Marshall, a tailor, looked out the window of his shop next door to the Custom House. Through the crowd, he spied a party of British soldiers and "saw their swords and bayonets glitter in the moonlight." Benjamin Burdick, who had left his house with his Scottish broadsword, headed toward the Town House, where a private named Hugh White stood behind seven grenadiers of the Twenty-ninth Regiment, under the command of Captain Thomas Preston. An hour earlier, White had left his sentry box to strike a young wigmaker's apprentice in the head with his musket, after the apprentice had taunted him by insulting a British officer who had failed to pay his wigmaker's bill. "Fire, damn you, fire!" the crowd goaded Preston. A bookseller named Henry Knox, just twenty years old, stepped forward and grabbed Preston's coat. "For God's sake, take care of your men," he pleaded. "If they fire, you die." "Are you loaded?" Burdick asked Hugh Montgomery, one of the grenadiers. Montgomery said yes. Lifting his broadsword, Burdick swung with all his might at Montgomery's musket. Montgomery stumbled, raised himself up from the ice, pulled the butt of his gun tight to his shoulder, and fired. "From that moment," Daniel Webster would later write, "we may date the severance of the British Empire."[44]

"The man on my left hand dropped," Burdick said, in a deposition he gave at Faneuil Hall that night. "I asked him if he was hurt, but received no answer, I then stooped down and saw him gasping and struggling with death." Crispus Attucks, a sailor, died from two bullet wounds in his chest. Attucks was a runaway slave. He had been advertised in the *Boston Gazette*, twenty years before:

Ran-away from his master *William Brown* of *Framingham* on the 30th of *Sept.* last a Mulatto Fellow about 27 Years of Age, named *Crispus*, 6 Feet and 2 Inches high, short curl'd Fair, his Knees nearer together than common; and had on a light colour'd Bearskin Coat, plain brown Fustian jacket, or brown all-Wool one, new Buckskin Breeches, blue Yarn Stockings and a checked woolen Shirt. Whoever shall take up said run-away and convey him to his aforesaid Master shall have *10 pounds* old Tenor Reward, and all necessary Charges paid. And all Masters of Vessels and others are hereby cautioned against concealing or carrying off said Servant on Penalty of Law.[45]

He was the first to die. Behind him, Samuel Gray spun and fell, his skull shattered by a bullet to the head. A bullet bounced off a wall and pierced the belly of seventeen-year-old Samuel Maverick. Two more shots felled an Irish sailor named James Caldwell. Patrick Carr, an apprentice leather worker, was hit by a musket ball that "went through his right hip & tore away part of the backbone."

When John Coburn, hearing the bells, had grabbed his fire buckets and knocked on a neighbor's door to rouse him, "He told me it was not a fire, it was a riot." Benjamin Burdick's wife, who, like Coburn's neighbor, had an uncanny and altogether suspicious foreknowledge that the bells rang for something other than fire, also called it an "affray," as did Phillis Wheatley, in a poem she wrote on the occasion, titled, "On the Affray in King Street." In the eighteenth century, an "affray" was akin to a "riot" (in 1757 Edmund Burke wrote of "the suppressing of riots and affrays"), while "massacre" meant then what it means now: the indiscriminate slaughter of a large number of innocent people. Five dead men—some of them armed with clubs and swords—do not a massacre make. But "massacre" it had to be, even though massacre it patently was not. Such, at least, was the conclusion reached by Samuel Adams sometime before eleven o'clock on the morning of Tuesday, March 6, when he, along with John Hancock and five more of the Sons of Liberty, drafted a report in which they called the soldiers' firing part of "a settled plot to massacre the inhabitants." Adams arranged for Edes to issue a pamphlet, *A Short Narrative of the Horrid Massacre in Boston*, and commissioned a ship to carry it to London. Paul Revere, meanwhile, engraved a picture of the scene, *The Bloody Massacre Perpetrated on King Street*, which Edes printed. It was a copy, really, of a drawing made by Copley's half brother, Henry Pelham. (Pelham, outraged by this act of plagiarism, wrote to Revere that it was "truly as if you had plundered me on the highway.") Like the *Horrid Massacre*, the *Bloody Massacre* overstated both the preparedness of the soldiers and the helplessness of the crowd. Revere's black-booted grenadiers are a well-regulated firing squad, flawlessly commanded from the rear by Preston, ordering them, with raised sword, to fire on a crowd of unarmed, middle-aged gentlemen, bewigged and bewildered. In many surviving copies, a colorist named Christian Remick has painstakingly painted the soldiers' coats red, a vividness balanced only by the shocking abundance of red blood spilling out of the wounds of the fallen men. Over the Custom House, Revere placed a sign reading "Butchers Hall," lest the verses that appeared below the illustration prove insufficiently explicit.

> Unhappy BOSTON see thy Sons deplore,
> Thy hallow'd Walks besmear'd with guiltless gore.
> While faithless P-----n and his savage Bands,
> With murd'rous Rancour stretch their bloody Hands;
> Like fierce Barbarians grinning o'er their Prey,
> Approve the Carnage and enjoy the Day.

On March 7, in a city of fifteen thousand people, twelve thousand showed up for the funeral of the massacre's first four victims (Patrick Carr still lingered), who were buried beneath a single gravestone, in the Old Granary Burying Ground, just steps from the Common. The "letter'd Stone shall tell," Wheatley wrote, "How Caldwell, Attucks, Gray, and Mav'rick fell."[46]

"All the government does is take my money and give it to other people," Austin Hess told me, the day of the Anti-Obamacare rally, in March of 2010. Hess's own salary was paid by the Departments of Defense and Homeland Security. He worked at MIT's Lincoln Laboratory, in Lexington, where he studied chemical and biological warfare. The next time I saw him, I asked him about that. "I'm not an anarchist," he said. "It's not that I think all government is bad."[47]

The remarkable debate about sovereignty and liberty that took place between 1761, when James Otis argued the writs of assistance case, and 1791, when the Bill of Rights was ratified, contains an ocean of ideas. You can fish almost anything out of it. (Almost anything, but not everything. There are fish that just weren't around in the eighteenth century, although that doesn't stop people from angling for them. Glenn Beck once said that George Washington was opposed to socialism.)[48] Tea Partiers liked to describe their movement as a catchall—Austin Hess identified himself as a libertarian, Christen Varley described herself as a social and fiscal conservative—but it didn't catch everything. Opposition to military power didn't have a place in the twenty-first-century Tea Party. It did, however, have a place in the Revolution, and also in its Bicentennial, which, before the Tea Party, was the last time so many Americans got so agitated about early American history.

In the 1960s, Lyndon Johnson's fifty-member American Revolution Bicentennial Commission didn't get much done. "My view is that the bicentennial should be a vehicle for social change," said Richard Barrett, an executive director of Johnson's commission. The study of African American history was on the rise. Colleges and universities had begun founding "black studies" departments. Bostonians had started a "Negroes' Freedom Trail." Black nationalists, though, thought the whole idea of celebrating American history was a travesty. "We didn't land on Plymouth Rock, my brothers and sisters," Malcolm X said. "Plymouth Rock landed on *us*." Johnson's commission wrestled with all this, without much success. When Nixon took office in 1969, Barrett left. The new administration, he said, "is not prepared to deal with the kind of problems I'd like to see dealt with." Then, too, by 1969, Martin Luther King Jr. was dead. So was Malcolm X. So were John F. Kennedy and Robert F. Kennedy. Was this really a good time to embrace revolution? The *New York Times* called the commission "hopelessly incompetent." Jesse Jackson called on black Americans to boycott the Bicentennial. To his own commission, Nixon appointed men who had worked on his campaign. Not long after, an antiwar activist named Jeremy Rifkin established a Peoples Bicentennial Commission, in protest, arguing that "in the 1970s the White House and Corporate America are planning to sell us a program of 'Plastic Liberty Bells,' red, white, and blue cars, and a 'Love It or Leave It Political Program.'"[49]

On May 4, 1970, the Ohio National Guard fired into a crowd of unarmed Kent State students protesting the U.S. invasion of Cambodia, killing four. This caused a lot of people to think about the Boston Massacre, not least because its two hundredth anniversary had only just passed. To a generation outraged by the Vietnam War, the argument against a standing army looked interesting, all over again. Amid the chaos, the Bicentennial was seized by the antiwar movement. After Kent State, college students papered their walls with posters of Revere's engraving.[50] The week after the shooting, a Kent State student told the *New York Times*, "They told King George or whoever that guy was, 'Look, leave us alone.' And he said no. And they said, 'Come on, leave us alone or there's going to be trouble.' And he still said no. So they said, 'All right, mother,' and they picked up a gun and started killing a bunch of British and tossing tea in the Boston harbor. And that's what's happening here."[51] In May of 1970, Howard Zinn was among about a hundred antiwar protesters arrested for blocking the road to a Boston army base. Brought to trial, Zinn told the court he was acting "in the grand tradition of the Boston Tea Party."[52] (Zinn's *People's History of the United States* is a product of the Bicentennial, too.) The following year, on Memorial Day weekend, hundreds of veterans marched, or wheeled their wheelchairs from Concord to Lexington, as if undertaking a piece of Paul Revere's ride in reverse. "This present hour in history is again a time when the people are trying to secure the liberty and peace upon which the country was founded," the Vietnam Veterans Against the War said. The National Park Service disagreed; its man in Lexington was sure that the "minutemen would be appalled." John Kerry said he wanted to "force the country to admit the mistake it has made in Indochina in the name of democracy." In Lexington, the veterans pitched camp on the Battle Green. Signs demanded the recall of the troops: "1781, Red Coats Go Home, 1971 Yankees Come Home."[53] People from the town handed out apples, sandwiches, sleeping bags, and blankets. In the morning, police in riot gear arrested five hundred people. Each veteran had agreed to give his "name, serial number, date of birth—April 18, 1775." Citizens from Lexington and Concord collected money to get the veterans out on bail. Back in Boston, veterans marched to Bunker Hill, where they laid down their arms—tossing toy guns into a pile—and then to the Common, where Senator Eugene McCarthy, the antiwar presidential candidate of 1968, gave a speech, telling the crowd that it was bearing witness to life and peace.[54] The time for revolution, they said, had come again.

"What ails the American spirit?" *Newsweek* asked, on the cover of its Fourth of July issue, in 1970. In the wake of Kent State, *Newsweek* posed that question to six historians. Yale's Staughton Lynd insisted that there was no such thing as an American spirit, but, except for that, no one quibbled with the question; everyone agreed that something was terribly wrong and that, whatever it was, it was unprecedented. The University of Rochester's Eugene Genovese declared "a state of spiritual crisis." Daniel Boorstin, later the librarian of Congress, offered a diagnosis of amnesia: "We have lost our sense of history." Andrew Hacker, then at Cornell, worried that the idea of citizenship was dead. Arthur Schlesinger Jr. stated the problem as "the velocity of history"; things were changing too much, too fast.

Richard Hofstadter's answer was bleakest. He was concerned that, in an increasingly secular age, young people on both the right and the left were bringing a religious zeal into politics: "This I think is a dangerous way of thinking, because when you try to get existential values out of politics, which has to do with wholly different things, I think you're heading for an increase in fanaticism." Kent State left Hofstadter despairing (he was also dying, at the age of fifty-three, of leukemia). "We'll be lucky to get out of this situation without further polarization and a strong right-wing reaction," he told *Newsweek*. "Part of our trouble is that our sense of ourselves hasn't diminished as much as it ought to."[55] Four months later, Richard Hofstadter was dead.

For all the periwigs, the Tea Party's Revolution, in the wake of Barack Obama's election, had very little to do with anything that happened in the 1770s. But it did have a great deal to do with what happened in the 1970s. The Tea Party's Revolution was the product of a reactionary—and fanatical—version of American history that took hold during the crisis over the Bicentennial, a reaction to protests from the left. That reactionary history simmered for decades and went, for the most part, unchallenged, because 1970 marked the end of an era in the writing of American history: Hofstadter would turn out to have been one of the last university professors of American history to reach readers outside the academy with sweeping interpretations both of the past and of his own time.

For much of its history, the American historical profession has defined itself by its dedication to the proposition that looking to the past to explain the present—and especially to solve present-day problems—falls outside the realm of serious historical inquiry. That stuff is for amateurs, toadies, and cranks. Historians decry the fallacy of "presentism": to see the past as nothing more than a prologue to the present introduces evidentiary and analytical distortions and risks reducing humanistic inquiry into shabby self-justification. Hofstadter recognized the perils of presentism, but he believed that historians with something to say about the relationship between the past and the present had an obligation to say it, as carefully as possible, by writing with method, perspective, skepticism, and an authority that derived not only from their discipline but also from their distance from the corridors of power. Schlesinger had left an appointment at Harvard to join the Kennedy administration; Hofstadter begged off a place in the Johnson administration; he would have found that unseemly.[56] (Schlesinger once wrote in his diary, "I am vaguely juxtaposed against Dick Hofstadter—the power-loving stablemate of statesmen as against the pure, dispassionate, incorruptible scholar," and then admitted, with admirable honesty, "There is something in this.") But, even if Hofstadter didn't defect from the university to the hurly-burly of politics, he found himself at odds with his colleagues. His knack for sweeping interpretation set him apart from his guild and earned him criticism, especially the captious kind. "The historians will have a field day with it," he wrote to a friend about one of his books, *The American Political Tradition*, "but I am in hopes that some of the non-academic people will like it."[57]

The Bicentennial—a carnival of presentism—helped make the position Hofstadter once occupied, which was always fragile, impossible. Historians mocked the Bicentennial as schlock and its protests as contrived but didn't offer an answer, a story, to a country that needed one.[58] That left plenty of room for a lot of other people to get into the history business.

CHAPTER 3

How to Commit Revolution

CONTAINING A SINGULAR ENCOUNTER WITH THE NATION'S
STORYTELLER—THE MISDAVENTURES OF MR. NIXON—A
FURTHER ACCOUNT OF THE PURSUIT OF LIBERTY—THE
TRAVELS OF PHILLIS WHEATLEY—A SPIRITED DEBATE AT
OLD SOUTH MEETING HOUSE—ACTS, INTOLERABLE—AND
MORE THAN ONE PARTY OF TEA

Shawn Ford used to work for a place called Paragon Tours
and Travel. Then he tried retail. One day in the 1980s, he was
laid off from his job at Jordan Marsh, a department store in
Downtown Crossing. "I walked to the Boston Common and
was sitting there drinking a Coke," he told me, "and a trolley
went by and I said, 'Well, that's something to do for the summer.'" He took a job at Old Town Trolley, with forty-three
trolleys, the largest sightseeing fleet in Boston, making four-
teen stops, including Faneuil Hall, the Old State House, and
Fenway Park, the oldest major league ballpark in the country.[1] Sometimes, Boston seems to be sinking under the weight
of its own history.

Old Town Trolley was owned by Historic Tours of America, a heritage-for-profit outfit founded in the 1970s by three
entrepreneurial Floridians who called their company "The
Nation's Storyteller." Historic Tours of America has hosted
two million visitors a year at attractions in six cities and sold

wares at twenty-five gift shops, or "historically themed retail environments." It was also the owner of the Boston Tea Party Ship, the *Beaver*, that boat that was tied up in Gloucester. Ford was vice president of international and domestic sales. I went to see him in March of 2010, in his office on the second floor of a warehouse on Dorchester Avenue in South Boston. Ford, nattily dressed, took me into a conference room to show me a promotional DVD about the plan for an ambitious expansion of the site on the Congress Street Bridge. Drum and fife music played during the opening scenes, over footage of the *Beaver*, before she was towed away.

"Today there are few symbols of American freedom more recognizable and compelling than the Boston Tea Party," said the narrator.

"Gosh, that guy's voice is really familiar," I said. "Who is that?"

Ford smiled. "Frank Avruch."

The name didn't ring a bell.

"Because of its significance to American history, and relevance to current events," Avruch went on, "the Boston Tea Party Ship and Museum has played a continuing role in political protests, education, historical interpretation, and the advancement of patriotic ideals."[2]

"Who?"

"He used to be Bozo the Clown," Ford said. Avruch was Bozo, on Boston television, in the 1970s.

After the *Beaver* gets back to Boston, Ford said, it will tell the story of "why we are such a great country."

"Our children have been taught to be ashamed of their country," Richard Nixon said, on January 20, 1973, in his second inaugural address. "At every turn, we have been beset by those who find everything wrong with America and little that is right." The Bicentennial could help fix that: "Let us pledge together to make these next four years the best four years in America's history, so that on its 200th birthday America will be as young and as vital as when it began."[3] Meanwhile, in *How to Commit Revolution American Style*, Jeremy Rifkin of the Peoples Bicentennial Commission was insisting, "It makes no sense for the New Left to allow the defenders of the system the advantage of presenting themselves as the true heirs and defenders of the American Revolutionary tradition. Instead, the revolutionary heritage must be used as a tactical weapon to isolate the existing institutions and those in power."[4]

And so it went, back and forth, the battle over the Revolution. Nixon, though, was distracted. Five men had broken into the Watergate hotel on June 17, 1972. Over the next weeks and months, an FBI investigation had tied the burglars to the Committee to Re-elect the President. As the two hundredth anniversary of the dumping of the tea approached, Nixon's Bicentennial Commission, mired in controversy, failed in every attempt to organize a national celebration. A $1.2 million plan to build a bicentennial park in all fifty states had been abandoned, as had plans for a world's fair to be held in Philadelphia. In Massachusetts, Kevin White, Boston's mayor, and a man with presidential aspirations, was determined to make the Bicentennial a highlight of his administration; he set up his own commission, Boston 200, and searched for corporate sponsors. That's when those three Boston businessmen bought an old Baltic schooner and had her refitted as an English brig, an undertaking funded by the makers of Salada Tea.

On the Fourth of July, 1973, the *New York Times* reported that an investigation into Nixon's Bicentennial Commission by the Government Accounting Office and the House Judiciary Committee had found a "startling lack of concrete ongoing programs."[5] That same day, at an event sponsored by another rival to Nixon's commission, the Afro-American Bicentennial Corporation, James Earl Jones read Frederick Douglass's 1852 speech, "The Meaning of July Fourth for the Negro," at Douglass's house, in Washington, DC:

> What, to the American slave, is your 4th of July? I answer; a day that reveals to him, more than all other days in the year, the gross injustice and cruelty to which he is the constant victim. To him, your celebration is a sham; your boasted liberty, an unholy license; your national greatness, swelling vanity; your sounds of rejoicing are empty and heartless; your denunciation of tyrants brass fronted impudence; your shouts of liberty and equality, hollow mockery; your prayers and hymns, your sermons and thanksgivings, with all your religious parade and solemnity, are to him, mere bombast, fraud, deception, impiety, and hypocrisy — a thin veil to cover up crimes which would disgrace a nation of savages.[6]

This, presumably, was just the kind of thing Nixon was talking about, this finding everything wrong with America. It wasn't invented by the New Left in the 1960s. It was quite old, in fact. Nixon's Bicentennial Commission wanted to offer a different history, one not only without Frederick Douglass but also at considerable variance with the best emerging scholarship, including the work of David Brion Davis, whose *The Problem of Slavery in the Age of Revolution* won the National Book Award in 1976, while Edmund S. Morgan's *American Slavery, American Freedom* was a runner-up.[7] But removing slavery from American history, even from eighteenth-century Boston, takes some doing, and means misunderstanding the

Revolution, not least because, as Davis and Morgan argued, slavery made liberty possible.

Two months after the Boston Massacre, John Hancock's uncle, the Reverend Samuel Cooke, delivered a sermon before the Massachusetts legislature, urging passage of the proposed antislavery bill: "We, the patrons of liberty . . . have dishonored the Christian name, and degraded human nature, nearly to a level with the beasts that perish. . . . Let not sordid gain, acquired by the merchandize of slaves, and the souls of men harden our hearts against her piteous moans. When God ariseth, and when he visiteth, what shall we answer!" Unfortunately, voting to end slavery threatened to undo what the Boston Massacre seemed, possibly, to be on the verge of accomplishing: unifying the colonies in their opposition to Parliament, and turning what looked to a lot of people to be Boston's fight into everyone's fight. And here, on this stark choice, everything seemed to turn. Either Boston, and Massachusetts, could join with England in the effort to abolish slavery (in 1772, England would end slavery, if vaguely, in the landmark *Somerset* case), or it could lead the colonies in the effort to resist parliamentary rule. Either the Sons of Liberty could choose to end slavery, or they could choose to battle Parliament. They could not do both. In 1771, when the antislavery bill finally came up for a vote, Mercy Otis Warren's husband, James, wrote to John Adams, "If passed into an act, it should have a bad effect on the union of the colonies." The bill failed.[8]

By now, James Otis was utterly lost. His mind, his sister wrote, was "clouded, shattered, and broken."[9] "British America will never prove undutiful till driven to it as the last fatal resort against an oppression that will make the weakest strong and the wisest mad," Otis had written, years before. This turned out to have been something of a prophecy. In 1771, Pelham wrote Copley about Otis, "At some times he is raving, at all times he is so bewildered as to have no dependence placed upon him."[10] A friend wrote to Mercy Otis Warren, "Perhaps Light may arise out of darkness, & he yet come forth as gold."[11] But Otis's sanity never returned. He spent most of the rest of his life locked up—his tortured, brief periods of lucidity even more painful than his madness. In these straits, Warren began answering her brother's letters. She felt that she had to do this, had to enter public life, even as a woman, because her brother had left it, with his work unfinished. She began allowing her writing to be published, anonymously. In 1772, she published a play called *The Adulateur*, which features a thinly disguised Thomas Hutchinson as a character named Rapatio. The next year, she published *The Defeat*, another political satire, in Edes's *Gazette*.[12]

Meanwhile, Boston's blacks looked to their own means to secure their freedom. In January of 1773, Felix, writing on behalf "of many Slaves, living in the Town of Boston, and other Towns in the Province," and probably with the support of members of the legislature, sent a letter to Hutchinson, begging for relief from bondage, which relief "to us will be as Life from the dead." In April, four black men from Boston submitted a petition for emancipation: "We expect great things from men who have made such a noble stand against the designs of their *fellow-men* to enslave them."[13] Phillis Wheatley, though, looked to England for her liberation. Preparing to cross the Atlantic, she had her portrait painted by Scipio Moorhead, a black painter who lived near the Town House. She secured a letter of reference, signed by gentlemen of Boston, including Thomas Hutchinson, John Hancock, and Andrew Eliot: "We whose names are under-written, do assure the World, that the Poems specified in the following Page, were (as we verily believe) written by PHILLIS, a young Negro Girl, who was but a few years since, brought an uncultivated barbarian from Africa." She sailed for London in May: "For thee *Britannia*, I resign / *New-England's* smiling fields." In July, the question at Harvard's graduation debate was "the Legality of Enslaving the Africans."[14] In an essay published that summer, Caesar Sartor, a former slave from Newburyport, pleaded: "Would you desire the preservation of your own liberty? As the first step let the oppressed Africans be liberated; then, and not till then, may you with confidence and consistency of conduct, look to Heaven for a blessing on your endeavours to knock the shackles . . . from your own feet."[15] In London, Wheatley met Benjamin Franklin. When Wheatley's *Poems on Various Subjects, Religious and Moral* was printed, not long after, she told this tale,

> . . . I, young in life, by seeming cruel fate
> Was snatch'd from *Afric's* fancy'd happy seat;
> What pangs excrutiating must molest,
> What sorrows labour in my parent's breast?
> Steel'd was that soul and by no misery mov'd
> That from a father seiz'd his babe belov'd:
> Such, such my case. And can I then but pray
> Others may never feel tyrannic sway?[16]

Reviewing Wheatley's book, one English critic wrote, "We are much concerned to find that this ingenious young woman is yet a slave. The people of Boston boast themselves chiefly on their principles of liberty. One such act as the purchase of her freedom would, in our opinion, have done more honour than hanging a thousand trees with ribbons and emblems."[17]

By then, though, everyone was quite concerned about tea. Parliament had repealed the Townshend Acts in 1770—all but the tax on tea. That year, three hundred wealthy Boston women had signed a pledge to stop drinking tea.[18] (Jane Mecom couldn't have afforded tea, anyway. She waxed philosophical. "I am convinced Poverty is Intailed on my Famely," she wrote that summer.)[19] In May of 1773, Parliament passed the Tea Act to bail out the East India Company, which, with a surplus of tea and stiff competition from smugglers, was facing bankruptcy. By eliminating duties on tea in England and lowering the import tax to just three pence, the Tea Act actually reduced the price of tea in the colonies, but it offended colonists, gravely, by its forceful assertion of Parliament's right to tax the colonies, and by its protection of a politically connected corporate monopoly. It wasn't the price; it was the principle. In June, letters written by Hutchinson, which Benjamin Franklin had acquired in London and leaked to friends in Boston, were published in Edes's *Gazette*. The Sons of Liberty began calling for Hutchinson's impeachment.

That summer, ships loaded with East India Company tea were sent to four cities: Boston, New York, Philadelphia, and Charleston. When Wheatley returned to Boston, in October of 1773, her owner granted her freedom. "I am now on my own footing," she wrote.[20] In November and December 1773, three tea ships, the *Beaver*, the *Eleanor*, and the *Dartmouth*, sailed into Boston Harbor (a fourth ship ran aground off Cape Cod). By law, they had twenty days to unload their cargo. The *Dartmouth*'s twenty days were set to expire at midnight on December 16. At ten o'clock that morning, seven thousand people showed up at Old South Meeting House to decide what to do. (Town meetings were usually held at

Faneuil Hall, but Old South was bigger, the biggest building in the city.) They debated for hours.

"The Boston Tea Party STARTED HERE" read a sign in Emily Curran's office. Curran, who resembled Emily Dickinson, was the director of Old South Meeting House. She grew up in Lexington. She was in high school in 1971 when half the town joined the Vietnam Veterans Against the War on the Battle Green and was hauled away in handcuffs. Curran had thought a lot about how to teach kids about stuff that happened in Boston in 1773, in a world very different, fundamentally different, from our own. The debate held in Old South on December 16, 1773, was restaged, most weekdays, by kids from the city's public schools. In the thoughtful program that Curran and her staff designed, the kids play parts.[21] "We don't have characters who wouldn't have been here," Curran told me. "So we have no women. Once I asked the kids, 'Why do you think all the roles you're playing today are men?' One girl raised her hand and said, confidently, 'Because there were no women back then.'" That, Curran said, was a good reminder of the work her staff has got cut out for it—measuring and marking out the distance between past and present.

Old South, a site on the Freedom Trail, only became a monument to the tea party in the 1870s. "Its primary claim to fame in the early 1800s wasn't the tea party," Curran said. "The Boston Massacre protest meetings were really a bigger and better remembered piece of the history of this building." During the hundredth anniversary of the dumping of the tea, in 1873, Ralph Waldo Emerson read his poem, "Boston," in Faneuil Hall:

> The cargo came! and who could blame
> If *Indians* seized the tea,

And, chest by chest, let down the same
Into the laughing sea?[22]

During those same festivities, though, Boston's mayor, Josiah Quincy, the grandson of a Son of Liberty, came close to disowning the entire affair. "We are not here today I think to glory over a mere act of violence, or a merely successful destruction of property . . . we know not exactly . . . whether any of the patriot leaders of the day had a hand in the act."[23] What saved Old South, Curran explained, wasn't the memory of the dumping of the tea but the demolition of John Hancock's mansion, in 1863, which occasioned outcry that the city was in danger of losing its history. In 1876, when Old South was scheduled to be torn down, a group of Bostonians got together to save the building, in New England's first ever effort at historic preservation. Old South was saved, not as an "idle shrine," its preservers insisted, but as a living site, for the working of democracy: free speech. Anyone could hold a meeting at Old South; in the last century, its board had granted permission to everyone from Sacco and Vanzetti supporters to neo-Nazis. In the 1920s, when dozens of books were "banned in Boston," Old South opened its doors to hold readings. Supporters of presidential aspirant Ron Paul once turned up in force. "I've been waiting for these Tea Party people to come," Curran told me, "but they haven't yet." She wasn't surprised by their interest in the Revolution, though. "Every group, it seems, can find a way to use the tea party for whatever cause they want."

One Wednesday in March of 2010, I watched a class of feisty fifth graders from the Marshall School in Dorchester duke it out at Old South. When the Marshall School opened in 1971, it enrolled seven hundred white and three hundred black students, and was, for its time and place, one of the most racially integrated schools in the district. In 1974, a federal circuit court mandated forced busing, to integrate Boston's public schools, which led first, to riots and then, to white flight. By 2008, the Marshall School was 58 percent black, 37 percent Hispanic, 2 percent white, and 1 percent Asian.[24]

"You are thirty-seven kids, and you need to sound like seven thousand people!" Zerah Jakub, of Old South's education program, told that class of fifth graders. "Mr. Samuel Adams, where are you?" she called. Up to the front stepped a tall, dark-skinned boy with glasses, to renounce the Tea Act. A tiny, willful girl played a shoemaker named George Robert Twelves Hewes: "Gentlemen, we cannot let the king and Parliament treat us like this." "Fie!" cried the little Loyalists. "King George treats us well . . . ," one girl whispered, from behind long brown bangs. "Don't we owe England our respect and support?" asked a girl with glasses, playing Peter Oliver. "But we did not get to vote on it," a kid with dimples pointed out. "Huzzah!" cried her side of the aisle. "What's stopping the king from raising it to four pence? Four pounds? Ten pounds?" asked Benjamin Edes. One of the teachers played Copley; he said he was "caught in the middle." After everyone had a turn, Jakub gave one of the kids a tricorn and a lantern and told him to go find the governor, because the people at Old South sent an emissary to Hutchinson, asking him to let the ships return to England without unloading the tea. When word came that Hutchinson had refused, the tall kid with glasses who was playing Samuel Adams shouted, "This meeting can do nothing more to save our country!" Thirty-seven fifth graders nearly blew the roof off: "Huzzah!"

Adams's shout may have been the signal for three groups of men, about fifty altogether, to head to the Green Dragon, the print shop of Edes's *Boston Gazette*, and a carpenter's house, where they disguised themselves as Mohawks, smearing their faces with soot. Then they marched to Griffin's Wharf, boarded the three ships, and dumped into the laughing sea three hundred chests of tea. More details about what happened that day and night are hard to come by. The night of the Boston Massacre, nearly one hundred people gave depositions; the Sons of Liberty were preparing a legal case, in order to charge Preston and his soldiers with murder. But the dumping the tea was, of course, a crime; the participants therefore pledged themselves to secrecy. Later—much later—people told stories about what happened and wrote memoirs. Some people kept souvenirs. When Thomas Melvill got home that night, he found some tea in his shoes and saved it. The next morning, an empty tea chest washed up on shore. Someone took it home.[25]

The Salada *Beaver* sailed from Denmark in May of 1973, just as the Watergate hearings got under way. In July, a witness revealed that Nixon had made tapes of conversations in the Oval Office. Archibald Cox, who headed the investigation, subpoenaed the tapes; Nixon refused to hand them over. The *Beaver* reached Massachusetts in October.[26] Nixon committed what the press called his "Saturday Night Massacre" on October 20, ordering first his attorney general, and next the deputy attorney general, to fire Cox. Both men refused, and resigned. Nixon then ordered his solicitor general, Robert Bork, to do the firing. Bork complied. "I'm not a crook," Nixon told reporters on November 17. On December 10, the *Boston Globe* covered its front page with an illustrated editorial titled "The Boston Tea Party . . . and this Generation":

Are we again today not made indignant by the abuse of power, violations of oaths of office, indifference to the public good, undermining of the people's confidence? Mishandling of problems, shortages, we all try to understand; none of us is perfect and great leaders are not always in abundant supply. But are we to tolerate longer publicly elected officeholders who do not belong exclusively to the entire public? It is not just the 18th century that tried men's souls. Our generation, too, has to act on democratic—and constitutional— principles in the face of arrogant use of power.[27]

Meanwhile, the city braced for Boston's "Tea Party Weekend," intended to be the kickoff of the Bicentennial, not just for Boston but for the whole country. It included a brunch, tea parties, a ball, and a great deal of gimcrackery: "Tea Party plates, tea boxes, Boston 200 brooch and teaspoon, Tea Party posters, silver and pewter Tea Party medallions, and Tea Party stamp cachets."[28] On the morning of December 16, twenty-five hundred people gathered at Faneuil Hall for a meeting held by the Peoples Bicentennial Commission, where Thomas Boylston Adams, a descendant of John Adams and president of the Massachusetts Historical Society, grieved for the state of the nation: "This should not be a day of commemoration but a day of mourning and prayer. We are faced today with the corruption, rot, arrogance and venality that our forefathers protested." Then everyone in the hall marched to the waterfront.[29] By noon, as falling snow turned to rain, forty thousand people gathered on Boston's bridges and wharves to watch the action on board the *Beaver*. "Dump Nixon, not tea" read one sign in the crowd. The National Organization for Women was there, picketing: "Taxation without Equal Rights Is Tyranny." Another banner read "Gay American Revolution." Rock music blared from loudspeakers. The ceremonies began at two o'clock when about thirty men wearing tricorns and knee breeches boarded the

Beaver. They were from the Charlestown Militia, a reenactment group founded by an Irish American longshoreman
named Jim O'Neil in 1967.[30] They dumped crates of tea into
the harbor. Minutes later, six protesters from the Peoples
Bicentennial Commission boarded the ship and unfurled a
flag reading "IMPEACH NIXON." (This, too, had been preap-
proved. "The bicentennial belongs to everyone," the people
at Boston 200 had always insisted.)[31] Then, as the Associated
Press reported,

> A member of the group, wearing a huge mask resembling
> President Nixon's face, circled the brig in a rowboat and
> waved his hands high in Nixon's familiar "V" style. That
> group also tarred and feathered a dummy of Nixon and
> hanged him in effigy. Members of the Disabled American
> Veterans, dressed as Indians, then boarded. . . . Genuine
> Indians, however, members of the Boston Indian Council,
> complained about the fakes.[32]

What happened in Boston that day made front-page news
across the country; it was reported in over two thousand
newspapers and magazines.[33] The coverage wasn't the kind
Kevin White wanted. "The first anguished attempt to make
something—anything" out of the Bicentennial, according to
an editorial in the *Washington Post*, was "distinguished by
commercial and ideological hucksterism." The whole thing,
including the protests, was "strained, self-conscious, artifi-
cially contrived" and "concocted."[34] Watergate made everything look bogus.

On March 21, 2010, the day of the House vote on the Patient
Protection and Affordable Health Care Act, Boston Tea Partiers held a vigil at the Green Dragon "to watch enemy troop

movements on C-SPAN," as Hess put it. "Seventeen seventy-three was all about taxation without representation," he had told me. This was only different because it was worse. "Can you imagine if the British said not only do you have to pay a tax on the tea, but you have to buy the tea and you have to buy tea for your neighbor?"

In the 1970s, Jeremy Rifkin's Peoples Bicentennial Commission started a tax-agitating Tea Party, too. The Peoples Bicentennial Commission published *America's Birthday: A Planning and Activity Guide for Citizens' Participation During the Bicentennial Years.* It called on ordinary Americans to form TEA Parties (the acronym stood for Tax Equity for Americans), because the country needed "a new party, a movement that will treat tax reform as one aspect of a fight for genuine equality of property and power and against taxation without representation." It urged TEA Party organizers to use the slogan "Don't Tread on Me." The book included step-by-step instructions:

> You might also consider staging your own events in places with captive audiences. How about a "King George Exhibit" of tax avoiders in some public park, with pictures and charts of the loopholes they use? How about forums on Tax Day, or on the anniversary of the Boston Tea Party—in front of IRS or H.&R. Block?[35]

"This is America in the '70s," Rifkin's favorite tagline went: "The 1770s and the 1970s."[36] Jeremy Rifkin wrote the Tea Party's playbook.

Austin Hess briefly thought about printing out a copy of the 2,400-page health care bill and dumping it into the harbor, but when he learned that would get him arrested, he decided against it. "We weren't ready for that," he told me. A lot of other junk has been dumped in Boston Harbor over the years, though. In 1988, the Just Say No days, a troop of Boy Scouts dumped a cask labeled "CRACK." Four years later, Teamsters meeting on Labor Day poured out cans of beer in the water and then tossed in the empty cases, though that sounds more like plain old littering. In 1997, a bunch of doctors and nurses, wearing scrubs, boarded the *Beaver* and threw overboard some HMOs' annual reports, thereby "launching a campaign against market-driven health care," according to the *Boston Globe*. House majority leader Dick Armey came to Boston in 1998 to unload a copy of the U.S. tax code. In 2007, state senators from Massachusetts, Texas, Georgia, and Virginia went to the wharf and dumped boxes bearing the labels of unfunded federal mandates, like No Child Left Behind, except they didn't actually dump them; that would be breaking the law. They pretended to dump them.[37]

"The Destruction of the Tea is so bold, so daring, so firm, intrepid and inflexible," John Adams wrote, "that I cant but consider it as an Epocha in history." A week after the dumping of the tea, he wrote to Mercy Otis Warren: "I wish to see a late glorious event celebrated by a certain poetical pen which has no equal that I know of in this country." (At the time, Adams and Warren were close friends.) He suggested the conceit. Warren, inspired, wrote the poem, called "The Squabble of the Sea Nymphs," after Pope's "Rape of the Lock," about a band of Indians who

> Pour'd a profusion of delicious teas,
> Which, wafted by a soft favonian breeze,
> Supply'd the wat'ry deities.

Adams arranged for it to be published in Edes's *Gazette*.[38] But for a while anyway, the dumping of the tea was less politically serviceable than what had happened three years before it. The Boston Massacre was commemorated every year from 1771 to 1783 with a public oration delivered before huge crowds. "Let all America join in one common prayer to heaven that the inhuman, unprovoked murders of the fifth of March . . . may ever stand on history without parallel," John Hancock said, when he gave the oration in 1774.[39] No one gave any speeches on the sixteenth of December. And no one called it a "tea party," either.[40] The dumping of the tea wasn't such a big deal. In 1823, the fiftieth anniversary of what had always been called, simply, "the destruction of the tea," passed without observance. Not so the rest of the semicentennial. The year 1825 saw the publication of the first historical novel set in Boston during the Revolution, Lydia Maria Child's *The Rebels*, and the laying of the cornerstone for the Bunker Hill monument. "Those who established our liberty and our government are daily dropping from among us," said Daniel Webster at the dedication.[41] The Revolutionary generation was dying. The next year, when news reached Boston that John Adams and Thomas Jefferson had died on the fiftieth anniversary of the Declaration of Independence, July, 4, 1826, all the ships in the harbor lowered their flags to half-mast.

In 1831, Oliver Wendell Holmes wrote a poem called "The Last Leaf," about Thomas Melvill, who was known around Boston as "the last of the cocked hats":

> I know it is a sin
> For me to sit and grin
> At him here;
> But the old three-cornered hat,
> And the breeches, and all that,
> Are so queer![42]

Melvill, the best-known surviving participant in the destruction of the tea, died in 1832. He was Herman Melville's grandfather. In Herman Melville's 1855 novel, *Israel Potter*, a hero of the Battle of Bunker Hill spends fifty years' exile in England, only to return to a Boston he can no longer understand (the book works much like Irving's "Rip Van Winkle"). In London, Potter meets the king, though he refuses to bow to him. "Immediately Israel touched his hat—but did not remove it." At the end of his exile, Potter, a man out of time, lands in Boston on the Fourth of July. He gets off the boat, walks up the wharf, and is nearly killed by the spirit of '75: "hustled by the riotous crowd near Faneuil Hall, the old man narrowly escaped being run over by a patriotic triumphal car in the procession, flying a broidered banner, inscribed with gilt letters:

'BUNKER HILL.
1775.
GLORY TO THE HEROES THAT FOUGHT!'"

He heads up to Copp's Hill, the burying ground behind the Old North Church, where he sits down, wearily, amid the gravestones. He wanders to places he once knew and finds that he doesn't know them anymore. He becomes a curiosity, a relic. Melville ends *Israel Potter* this way: "He dictated a little book, the record of his fortune. But long ago it faded out of print—himself out of being—his name out of memory."[43]

What happened in Boston in 1773 was first called a "tea party," at least in print, in the title of a book published in 1834: *A Retrospect of the Boston Tea-Party: With a Memoir of George R. T. Hewes*. Hewes, a poor shoemaker, has much in common with Israel Potter. He was, after Melvill's death, one of the last surviving participants of the destruction of the tea. In 1835, Hewes, now in his nineties, was brought to Boston for a Fourth of July parade. Calling the dumping of the tea a "tea party" made it sound like a political party: in the 1770s, parties were anathema ("If I could not go to heaven but with a party," Jefferson wrote, "I would not go there at all"), but in the 1830s, parties ran politics—and fought over who carried the mantle of the passing Revolutionary generation. By parading Hewes through the streets of the city, Boston's Whigs, who, after all, had named their party after the patriots, claimed the so-called Tea Party as their own.[44]

Meanwhile, what the Revolution meant to Hewes—that a poor man was as good a man as any other—was lost. In 1762, when Hewes was a twenty-year-old apprentice, he repaired a shoe for John Hancock, the richest man in Boston. On New Year's Day, in one of the era's many elaborate rituals of deference to rank and wealth, Hewes went to Hancock's house, the grandest mansion in the city, met the great man, took off his hat, bowed, and was given a coin. In 1778, Hewes, still as poor as dirt, enlisted to serve on board the *Hancock*, a twenty-gun ship, to fight the British. But when a ship's officer demanded that Hewes doff his hat to him, Hewes would not. He refused, he said, to doff his hat for any man.[45]

"We don't have a problem with the sites on the Freedom Trail," Shawn Ford told me, after we sat down in his office, "but they have a problem with us." Historic Tours of America began operating the Boston Tea Party Ship in 1988 and bought it six years later. The attraction had not often been celebrated for its educational value. ("It became about making money," Curran told me. "Interpretive decisions were based on that.") Ford talked about the company's commitment to the visitor's experience. "Running a for-profit attraction is a lot more difficult than a nonprofit. How we pay for this is the guest that comes through the front door."

When the site was damaged by fire, Historic Tours of America determined that the entire attraction was due for a renovation and hired Leon Poindexter, a master shipwright, to gut the *Beaver* and rebuild it. The plan was to reopen the Congress Bridge site with replicas of all three ships docked on a barge, the foundation for a museum. Poindexter, one of the few remaining people in the world who knew how to build an eighteenth-century ocean-faring vessel, had worked on many ships, including those in the film *Master and Commander.* He put a great deal of painstaking work into the renovation of the *Beaver.* In 2005, he also began taking apart an old fishing boat and turning it into the *Eleanor,* which was docked alongside the *Beaver,* in Gloucester. Poindexter hadn't started on the third ship, the *Dartmouth,* when Historic Tours of America ran out of money; then, in 2007, came the second fire at the Congress Street site and, in 2008, the credit crunch dried up any chance of a new loan.

The plan was now back on track, Ford said. He brought out a handsome architect's model, placed it on his desk, and walked me through the "three-stage experience" of what would be called the Boston Tea Party Ships and Museum. Stage 1: "You enter the meeting house. It will look as if they're in Old South. We call this a 'faux reenactment.' There will be actors in period costume." That is, the entrance to this for-profit attraction would be a re-creation of the Old South Meeting House, an original eighteenth-century building still standing, not a half mile away, open to the public, and operated as a nonprofit, as a sanctuary for free speech.

Stage 2: "You march down the ramp and get on the *Beaver* or the *Eleanor*. Then go below decks to see what ship life was like." The plan was for the *Dartmouth* to be built on site, its construction an exhibit in itself. Stage 3: "The museum is still being designed. There will be a theater." There would be a film: "the tea party as seen through the eyes of a tea crate."

Historic Tours of America catered mostly to older Americans, "aging Baby Boomers," its company profile said. It sold celebration. For that generation, the struggle for civil rights, the tragedy of Vietnam, and the betrayals of Watergate made patriotism a sorrow. Heritage tourism provided a balm.

On Sunday, March 21, 2010, the U.S. House of Representatives passed the health care bill, in a vote that fell along partisan lines. All but 34 Democrats voted for it, and all 178 Republicans voted against it. On Monday, eleven state attorneys general announced a plan to challenge the law as a violation of state sovereignty. Across the country, there followed scattered threats of violence against legislators who had voted in favor of the bill and against the president who signed it into law on Tuesday, by which time there had already been talk of nullification.

The next night, I met Austin Hess and Kat Malone at the Warren Tavern in Charlestown. The tavern, built in 1784, was named after Dr. Joseph Warren, who died in the Battle of Bunker Hill, and was just a cobbled street away from Monument Square, where a granite obelisk commemorated the patriots who died alongside him. We sat near the bar, beneath a dark ceiling of massive oak timbers. Tin lanterns hung from the wall. Hess took off his tricornered hat and set it down on the table between us. Malone was quiet. Hess was frustrated. "I have recently started a committee to elect the corpse of Calvin Coolidge," he said, "because anyone's better than Obama." He was dismayed by the vote, but he was also, as always, courteous and equable. "It's the law of the land now, so, it's up to us to blunt its impact and overturn it if we can." The vote, and House Speaker Nancy Pelosi's maneuvering around a potential filibuster made possible by Brown's election to the Senate, had deepened Hess's conviction about the aptness of his analogy. "One of the things people like to say about us is that they like to think that we don't know what we're talking about, that we don't know what the tea party was about. But to the people who say we have taxation with representation, I would just say that they should look to the bill that just passed. We sent Scott Brown to Washington to kill this bill, but the people in Washington did everything they could to thwart the will of the people, and especially the people of Massachusetts. How is my voice being represented?"

In 1774, in response to the dumping of the tea, Parliament passed what colonists called the Intolerable Acts: the Boston Port Act closed the port; the Massachusetts Government Act greatly constrained the activities of town meetings. Hutchinson was removed as governor; General Thomas Gage, commander of the British forces in America, was appointed in his place. (The legislature had actually voted to impeach Hutchinson earlier, following the publication of the Hutchinson letters leaked by Franklin.) A secret society of men, including Revere, Hancock, Warren, and the Adamses, met at the Green Dragon "for the purpose of watching the British soldiers," as Revere wrote.[46] Hutchinson sailed for England in May; Copley followed him shortly afterward. "Mr. Copley may be looked upon as the Greatest Painter we have ever yet had in America," an admirer wrote, just months before

Copley set sail. (Copley never returned. He died in 1815 and is buried in London.)[47]

The port was closed on the first of June; the only ships to arrive in Boston were those carrying still more British soldiers. In August, John and Samuel Adams set off, by carriage, for Philadelphia, for the first meeting of the Continental Congress. "The distinction between Virginians, Pennsylvanians, New Yorkers, and New Englanders, are no more," Patrick Henry declared in Philadelphia. "I am not a Virginian, but an American."[48]

Not long after, a man named Thomas Pain washed up in Philadelphia. Pain was born in Thetford, England, in 1737 (he added the *e* later, and was called "Tom" only by his enemies), the son of a Quaker journeyman who sewed the bones of whales into stays for ladies' corsets. He left the local grammar school at the age of twelve to serve as his father's apprentice. At twenty, he went to sea, on a privateer. In 1759 he opened his own stay-making shop and married a servant girl, but the next year both she and their child died in childbirth. For a decade, Pain struggled to make a life for himself. He taught school, collected taxes, and, in 1771, married a grocer's daughter. Three years later, he was fired from his job with the excise office; his unhappy and childless second marriage fell apart; and everything he owned was sold at auction to pay off his debts. At the age of thirty-seven, Thomas Pain was ruined. He therefore did what every ruined Englishman did, if he possibly could: he sailed to America. Sickened with typhus during the journey, Pain arrived in Philadelphia in 1774 so weak he had to be carried off the ship. What saved his life was a letter found in his pocket: "The bearer Mr Thomas Pain is very well recommended to me as an ingenious worthy young man."[49] It was signed by Benjamin Franklin. It was better than a bag of gold.

In Massachusetts, the people stockpiled weapons in the countryside. In September, after Gage seized ammunition stored in Charlestown and Cambridge, the legislature established a Committee of Safety; in October, it created special units of "minutemen," who could be ready to fight at a moment's notice. "The people trembled for their liberties, the merchant for his interest, the tories for their places, the whigs for their country," wrote Mercy Otis Warren.[50] Josiah Quincy Jr. cried: "I speak it with grief, I speak it with anguish. Britons are our oppressors: I speak it with shame, I speak it with indignation: *we are slaves.*"[51] "For shame," preached a Massachusetts minister, "let us either cease to enslave our fellowmen, or else let us cease to complain of those that would enslave us."[52] Twelve days after Gage took office, he received a letter from "a Grate Number of Blackes," who demanded their liberty, presumably on the theory, why not try the British? "We have in commen With all other men a naturel right to our freedoms without Being depriv'd of them by our fellow men as we are a freeborn Pepel."[53] Abigail Adams wrote to John in Philadelphia about "a conspiracy of the negroes" in September 1774; they had prepared "a petition to the Governor, telling him they would fight for him provided he would arm them and engage to liberate them if he conquered" the local rebels. ("I wish most sincerely there was not a slave in the province," she added. "It always appeared a most iniquitous scheme to me—to fight ourselves for what we are daily robbing and plundering from those who have as good a right to freedom as we have.")[54]

In London, Samuel Johnson wrote a pamphlet called *Taxation No Tyranny*, in which he asked, "How is it that we hear the loudest yelps for liberty among the drivers of negroes?"[55] Meanwhile, in Boston, Wheatley wrote in a letter that was widely published, "In every human breast, God has implanted a Principle, which we call Love of Freedom; it is impatient of Oppression, and pants for Deliverance." She offered her own remarks about the nature of hypocrisy. "How well the Cry for Liberty and the reverse Disposition for the Exercise of oppressive Power over others agree I humbly think it does not require the Penetration of a Philosopher to determine."[56]

In March of 1775, Patrick Henry gave a yet more stirring speech: "Is life so dear, or peace so sweet, as to be purchased at the price of chains and slavery? Forbid it, Almighty God! I know not what course others may take; but as for me, give me liberty or give me death!" The following November, Virginia's royal governor, Lord Dunmore, offered freedom to any slaves who would join His Majesty's troops in suppressing the American rebellion. Dunmore's proclamation would animate the passions of George Washington's own slaves. "There is not a man of them but would leave us if they believed they could make their escape," Washington's cousin wrote from Mount Vernon, adding bitterly, "Liberty is sweet."[57]

"I really feel like this is a modern-day Intolerable Act," Austin Hess said, about the new health care law, when we met at the Warren Tavern. Every time Hess talked about the Intolerable Acts, I got to thinking about the limits of tolerance, tolerance of racial equality, of religious diversity, of same-sex marriage, of a global economy, of democracy, of pluralism, of change. Hess labored in a world of uneasy alliances. I asked him if he was troubled by Christen Varley's work with the Coalition for Marriage and the Family. "We do not discuss social issues and foreign policy issues," he said. He was frustrated that journalists kept getting the Tea Party wrong.

Hess's girlfriend was black. He was tired of people calling the movement racist. "I will simply say this," he e-mailed me. "I know what is in my heart."[58]

In 2010, nationwide polls reported that people who identified themselves as sympathetic with the Tea Party were overwhelmingly white, although estimates varied, and the Tea Party didn't appear to be much whiter than, say, the Republican Party.[59] Whatever else had drawn people into the movement—the bailout, health care, taxes, Fox News, and, above all, the economy—some of it, for some people, was probably discomfort with the United States' first black president, because he was black. But it wasn't the whiteness of the Tea Party that I found most striking. It was the whiteness of their Revolution. The Founding Fathers were the whites of their eyes, a fantasy of an America before race, *without* race. There were very few black people in the Tea Party, but there were no black people at all in the Tea Party's eighteenth century. Nor, for that matter, were there any women, aside from Abigail Adams, and no slavery, poverty, ignorance, insanity, sickness, or misery. Nor was there any art, literature, sex, pleasure, or humor. There were only the Founding Fathers with their white wigs, wearing their three-cornered hats, in their Christian nation, revolting against taxes, and defending their right to bear arms.

"The first book I brought home from kindergarten was about George Washington," Hess told me. "I made my mother read it to me, the whole thing." Like Beck, Hess believed that the teaching of American history in the nation's public schools had been corrupted by ideologues from the left. (One of the more bizarre things about this was that the far right, in rejecting historical scholarship as a conspiracy of the left, had conflated the hucksterism of Jeremy Rifkin's

Peoples Bicentennial Commission with the distinguished research and writing of the century's best historians, including Edmund Morgan, as if Morgan's attempt to desegregate American history, to weave together the stories of liberty and slavery, were the same as Rifkin's specious comparisons of OPEC and the East India Company.) Hess believed that he had resisted the left-wing indoctrination that was part of his public schooling. "As much as the textbooks we read in school were biased in favor of the New Deal, I was never really sold on it," he said.

The scholarship academic historians have written since the 1960s, uncovering the lives of ordinary people and examining conflict among groups and especially races, sexes, classes, and nations, was not without substantial shortcomings. Critics, both within and outside the academy, had charged scholars of American history not only with an inability to write for general readers and an unwillingness to examine the relationship between the past and the present, but also with a failure to provide a narrative synthesis, to tell a big story instead of many little ones. Those criticisms were warranted. They were also criticisms academic historians had made of themselves. Scholars criticize and argue— and must, and can—because scholars share a common set of ideas about how to argue, and what counts as evidence. But the far right's American history—its antihistory—existed outside of argument and had no interest in evidence. It was much a fiction as the Lost Cause of the Confederacy, reductive, unitary, and, finally, dangerously antipluralist.[60] It erased slavery from American history and compressed a quarter century of political contest into "the founding," as if ideas worked out, over decades of debate and fierce disagreement, were held by everyone, from the start. "Who's your favorite Founder?" Glenn Beck asked Sarah Palin. "Um, you know, well," she said. "All of them."[61]

There was, though, something heartbreaking in all this. Behind the Tea Party's Revolution lay nostalgia for an imagined time—the 1950s, maybe, or the 1940s—less riven by strife, less troubled by conflict, less riddled with ambiguity, less divided by race. In that nostalgia was the remembrance of childhood, a yearning for a common past, bulwark against a divided present, comfort against an uncertain future. "History is not a dry academic subject for us," as Hess put it. "It is our heritage."[62]

CHAPTER 4

The Past upon Its Throne

CONTAINING AN EVENING AT THE GREEN DRAGON TAVERN—
PAUL REVERE, AT A CLIP-CLOP—SCENES OF BATTLE—THE
ARRIVAL OF GENERAL WASHINGTON—A SHORT HISTORY
OF THE BALLOT—CONSTITUTIONAL COMPROMISES—THE
ARGUMENT OF MR. LINCOLN—THE END OF AN UNPOPULAR
WAR—MATTERS OF FAITH—AND REMARKS ON THE ORIGINS
OF ORIGINALISM

On Thursday, April 8, 2010, the Boston Tea Party held its regular monthly meeting in the Green Dragon Tavern, and the *Boston Phoenix* ran a cover story called "Tea Is for Terrorism."[1] There had been a great deal of talk at the last Green Dragon meeting about the importance of drawing the line between the real Tea Party and the crackpots. "I mean, when you see the picture of Obama with the Hitler mustache, it's clear," Varley had said. "Those are the LaRouche people." So I kept thinking that more of the people I had met would distinguish their positions from the conspiracy theories that prevailed in and around the Tea Party, nationally—the "Birthers'" insistence that Barack Obama is not an American citizen, for instance—theories with which many of the people I had met did, in fact, disagree. Austin Hess had told me that during that very first Tax Day rally, on April 15, 2009, a reporter had come up to him and said, "So, do you hate Obama because he's a Muslim?" Hess said he thought, "Huh? Obama's not a Muslim." He found the question maddening. "There will always be nuts who show up, but they don't reflect the views of the movement," he explained. But at that same rally, a featured speaker, talking about the president, goaded the audience, "When he informs us that we are no longer a Christian nation, are you going to go along with that?" ("No!" the crowd called back.) Varley didn't want anyone holding Hitler signs, but at the Fourth of July rally she organized in 2009, an invited speaker rambled on about the "growing quasi-uber-state" and spoke of a "fascist government."[2] In the Tea Party, the fringe wasn't some shifty-looking riffraff carrying a creepy sign; it was the loudmouth holding the microphone.

By now, word about Sarah Palin's visit had gotten around. Two buses from the Maine Tea Party were already confirmed. Twenty thousand people might turn up, forty thousand. Who knew? But there was every reason to believe that the rally would also draw counterprotesters. Someone passed around a copy of the *Dig*, a free Boston weekly, which had sponsored an anti-Palin poster contest. "Oh No, I can see Sarah Palin From My Back Yard," read one submission. Another:

TEA PARTIES.
OURS: REAL.
YOURS: BULL.[3]

I sat down with George Egan, the retired cop I'd met the month before, and his twin brothers, John and Joe. Their grandparents came over from Ireland in 1907. The Egan brothers grew up in Dorchester. They thought Palin was a pain. They couldn't stomach former Massachusetts governor and presidential aspirant Mitt Romney, either. "I can't wait to see how he's going to lie his way out of Romneycare," Joe said. George, kindly offering to explain to me, once again, his position on health care, told me this story: "My little girl, when she was three, she got real sick. Had to be in intensive care for ten days. Had to have a tracheotomy. I had shit for insurance. The hospital sent me a bill. Ten thousand dollars. I got a second job; I sent the hospital one hundred bucks a month. That was the right thing to do. This is wrong. People want something, they have to work for it."

George and Joe and John Egan had worked very hard, all their lives. They were mad about the bums—the bums on the streets, the bums in Washington. George said, "Every drug addict gets a check. We write those checks." Joe said, "Stay out of our wallets. I don't care: Democrat, Republican? I don't care. Just less of them." The Egans were some of only a handful of Boston Tea Partiers I met who were actually born in Massachusetts. They reminded me of a lot of people I've known all my life. The house where I grew up was a lot like the Egans's, but Hess, who was wearing his "Don't Tread on Me" T-shirt, figured me for a foreigner. "Jane Goodall, meet the man who's going to beat Barney Frank," he said, introducing me to Sean Bielat, who was running for Frank's seat, as a Massachusetts member of the U.S. House of Representatives, in the fall elections. "She's going to make a contribution to your campaign," Joe Egan joked when I started scribbling notes on Bielat's campaign brochure. "Really?" Bielat asked, lighting up. "No, of course not," George said. "She's from the People's Republic of Cambridge." Bielat wandered off.

On April 14, 1775, General Thomas Gage received orders from London to arrest the leaders of the rebellion, the men who met at the Green Dragon Tavern.[4] On a list of rebels who, the minute war broke out, were to be shot on sight, appeared a postscript: "N.B. Don't forget those trumpeters of sedition, the printers Edes and Gill."[5] The Sons of Liberty went into hiding. On April 18, Joseph Warren, hearing that Gage planned to march to Lexington and Concord to seize the colonists' stores of arms, gave Paul Revere and William Dawes orders to sound the alarm. After a lantern at the Old North Church gave the signal, Revere began his ride to warn everyone—including Hancock and Samuel Adams, who were in hiding in Lexington—that the redcoats were coming. "I set off upon a very good Horse; it was then about 11 o'Clock," Revere later recalled, and soon "got nearly opposite where Mark was hung in chains."[6] (Even all those years later, the site of that slave's execution remained a landmark.) Revere didn't issue this warning alone; he was aided by boatmen who rowed him across the Charles, by messengers who met him along the way, and by militiamen, who helped spread the word across the countryside, long before Revere got there. He reached Lexington about one in the morning and was then detained by British troops blocking the road to Concord. He wasn't the only one to rush out of the city. Back in Boston, Benjamin Edes and John Gill hastily dissolved their partnership. Gill went into hiding. Under cover of darkness, Edes, alone, carted his printing press and types to the Charles River, where he loaded them onto a boat moored at the bank and rowed through the night.[7]

At daybreak, some seven hundred redcoats reached Lexington, where they found about seventy armed minutemen waiting for them. "Lay down your arms, you damned rebels, and disperse!" one British officer shouted. Outnumbered, the minutemen began to retreat. "Damn you, why don't you lay down your arms!" The British fired, killing eight. They marched on to Concord where Reverend William Emerson had called out the minutemen, urging them: "If we die, let us die here." Two minutemen did die that day—"Twas for the future that they fought," the poet James Russell Lowell once wrote—and, at Concord Bridge, three British soldiers fell. Lowell once visited the redcoats' graves, and wrote:

> They came three thousand miles, and died
> To keep the Past upon its throne.[8]

Boston, occupied by the British and surrounded by the colonial militia, was now a city under siege. Thousands fled. Sixty-three-year-old Jane Mecom packed what she could onto a wagon. (She ended up in Rhode Island, until, in the fall, Benjamin Franklin, upon his return from London, traveled to Washington's headquarters in Cambridge and brought his sister back to Philadelphia with him.)[9] Andrew Eliot grieved. "The unhappy situation of this town, which, by the late cruel and oppressive measures gone into by the British Parliament, is now almost depopulated," he wrote. His wife and eight of his children fled, but Eliot felt he had no choice but to stay in Boston to preach to those left behind: "Nothing keeps me from leaving the town but the obligation I am laid under not to leave so many people without ordinances."[10] Of a population of fifteen thousand there were, in a matter of days, only three thousand people left in the city. Most were loyalists, like Henry Pelham, who wrote to Copley of "all the Horrors of a Civil War." British troops gutted the Old South Meeting House, burned the pews and pulpit, and used the floor to exercise their horses. They chopped down the Liberty Tree and used it for fuel. A party of soldiers broke into Edes's print shop on Queen Street, and, failing to find him, they seized his son instead. Eighteen-year-old Peter Edes spent months as a prisoner of war. He watched from the window of his cell while a fellow captive, a Boston painter, was dragged to the yard and beaten until, broken, he finally called out, "God bless the King."[11]

Across the river in Watertown, Benjamin Edes set up a makeshift printing shop, with whatever supplies he could find. On June 5, he started publishing the *Gazette* again, on lumpy paper, with gunky ink. In Cambridge, Harvard students were sent home. Some seven hundred American soldiers were quartered in Massachusetts Hall, in Harvard Yard. The contents of Harvard's library were carried to Andover for safekeeping.[12] John Hancock and John and Samuel Adams headed to Philadelphia, to the Second Continental Congress, which convened on May 10. Hancock was elected president; John Adams nominated George Washington to command a Continental army. Even as Washington rode northward, American forces outside Boston, learning that Gage planned to take a hill outside the city, decided to try to hold a line at Charlestown, on Breed's Hill. On June 17, shots were fired in what came to be called the Battle of Bunker Hill. Lost in that battle were 140 Americans, including Joseph Warren, and 226 British. ("Don't fire until you see the whites of their eyes!" is the order allegedly given by Israel Putnam to the colonial militiamen. But there's not much evidence Putnam ever said that. That story comes from Parson Weems and didn't enter textbooks until the Civil War.)[13] The Americans had more than proved their mettle, but they lost the hill. The British burned Charlestown to the ground. "Town consumed. oh!" Andrew Eliot wrote, frantically, in the almanac that served as his diary, where he recalled Virgil: "Diem horrendum! bella horrida bella!"[14]

On July 3, 1775, George Washington took command of the Continental army on the Cambridge Common. In 1875, on the one hundredth anniversary of that day, James Russell Lowell read a poem, on that same spot—"Here, where we stand, stood he"—about "the seamless tapestry of thought . . . that binds all ages past with all that are to be."[15]

After Sean Bielat learned that I was from Cambridge and moved to the next table, I asked Austin Hess what he thought would happen in the midterm congressional elections in the fall. "November will be a bloodbath," he said, confident of an anti-incumbency victory at the ballot box. I'm not sure about the seamless tapestry of thought that binds all ages past with all that are to be, but historians do like to think about where things come from, including things like ballots and universal suffrage, which are more things that, if we were getting back to what the founders had, we wouldn't have.

On Election Day every November, I walk around the corner to vote in the basement gymnasium of a neighborhood elementary school, beneath a canopy of basketball hoops. At a table just inside the gym, a precinct volunteer hands me a piece of white paper about the size and weight of a file folder. I enter a booth built of aluminum poles, tug shut behind me a red-, white-, and blue-striped curtain, and, with a black marker tied by a string to a tabletop, I mark my ballot, awed, every time, by the gravity, the sovereignty, of the moment. That I vote, and almost everything about how I vote, was unimaginable by the Founding Fathers.

The word "ballot" comes from the Italian *ballota*, or ball, and in the 1600s, a ballot usually was a ball, or at least something ball-ish, like a pea or a pebble, or, not uncommonly, a bullet. Colonial Pennsylvanians voted by tossing beans into a hat. Elsewhere, people voted with their voices—*viva voce*—or with their hands or, literally, with their feet, walking to different sides of a room, or a town common, for different candidates. Every town, county, and colony, and later, every state, determined its own method of voting. Casting a vote only rarely required paper and pen. Everyone knew how everyone else voted. Casting a "secret ballot" was considered cowardly, underhanded, and despicable. Paper voting, when it started, wasn't meant to conceal anyone's vote; it was just easier than counting beans.[16]

The first recorded colonial use of paper voting comes from Massachusetts: in 1629, church members in Salem elected their pastor by writing his name down on slivers of parchment. In 1634, John Winthrop, the colony's first governor, was elected "by paper"; thirteen years later, a Bay Colony law dictated voting "by wrighting the names of the persons Elected."[17] The federal Constitution of 1787 left the conduct of elections up to the states: "The times, places and manner of holding elections for Senators and Representatives, shall be prescribed in each state by the legislature thereof; but the Congress may at any time by law make or alter such regulations." Further than this limited federal oversight the framers would not go. And even this needed Madison's insistence, during the Constitutional Convention, that "it was impossible to foresee all the abuses" that states might make of unimpeded power over the conduct of elections.[18]

And, of course, in establishing the federal government, the Constitution made a compromise on the fundamental question about suffrage that had started the Revolution in the first place: taxation without representation. How were the people to be represented? Should the states, big and small, have equal representation in Congress, or should they be represented according to their size? Madison argued that the states were divided "not by their difference of size . . . but principally from the effects of their having or not having slaves." Over this question, South Carolina threatened to walk out, one of its delegates declaring, "You must give each state an equal suffrage, or our business is at an end." At a dinner meeting at his house, Benjamin Franklin proposed what became known as the Connecticut Compromise. In the Senate, states would have equal representation; in the lower house, representation would be proportionate to population, one representative for every forty thousand free people; slaves would count as three-fifths of a person. Only the lower house would have the power to tax. The three-fifths clause held the country together, by perpetuating an institution many delegates to the convention despised. Its consequences were horrible to contemplate. "What will be said of founding a Right to govern freemen on a power derived from slaves"? was the question posed by John Dickinson. Gouverneur Morris stated it squarely: "The admission of slaves into the representation, when fairly explained, comes to this: that the inhabitant of Georgia and South Carolina who goes to the coast of Africa and, in defiance of the most sacred laws of humanity, tears away his fellow creatures from their dearest connections and damns them to the most cruel bondage, shall have more votes in a government instituted for protection of the rights of mankind than the citizen of Pennsylvania or New Jersey who views with a laudable horror so nefarious a practice." At the end of the convention, George Washington went home to Virginia and began laying a plan to manumit his slaves.[19]

In the Constitution written in Philadelphia, taxation, representation, and slavery were entirely tangled together.[20] Voting, itself, was left to the states. The Constitution makes no provision for how Americans should vote, not only because the men who wrote it wanted to leave such matters (mostly) to the states but also because, as only Madison glimpsed, they could not possibly have foreseen how unwieldy elections would very soon become. With the exception of Franklin, who anticipated Malthus, the men who met in Philadelphia could scarcely have imagined that the population of the United States, less than four million in 1790, would increase, tenfold, by 1870. Nor did they prophesy the party system. Above all, they could not have fathomed universal suffrage, which entirely defied eighteenth-century political philosophy. The popular will had to be restrained, sifted, as if through a sieve. The framers expected only a tiny minority of Americans to vote. And these men wouldn't elect the president directly; they would vote only for electors of the Electoral College, an institution established to further restrain the popular will.[21]

The states, left to their own, adopted electoral methods best described as higgledy-piggledy. Five of the original thirteen state constitutions made mention of voting by ballot.[22] "An opinion hath long prevailed among diverse good people of this state," wrote the framers of New York's 1777 Constitution, "that voting at elections by ballot would tend more to preserve the liberty and freedom of the people than voting *viva voce*"; they proposed a "fair experiment" with the paper ballot.[23] In 1799, Maryland became the first state to require paper voting in all statewide elections. The Twelfth Amendment, ratified in 1804, mandated that members of the Electoral College "vote by ballot." By no means, however, did paper voting become universal. The citizens of Kentucky voted *viva voce* until 1891.

Early paper voting was, to say the least, a hassle. You had to bring your own ballot, a scrap of paper. Then you had to

(a) remember and (b) know how to spell the names and titles of every candidate and office. If "John H. Jones" was standing for election and you wrote "John Jones," your vote would be thrown out. (If you doubt how difficult this is, try it. I disenfranchise myself at "comptroller.") Shrewd partisans began bringing prewritten ballots to the polls and handing them out . . . with a coin or two. Doling out cash—the money was called "soap"—wasn't illegal; it was getting out the vote.

Meanwhile, the eighteenth-century's brilliant experiment in republicanism gave way to the unruly exuberance of nineteenth-century democracy. New states entering the union adopted constitutions without any property qualifications for voting, putting pressure on older states to eliminate those restrictions. The electorate doubled and then tripled. And still it kept growing. As suffrage expanded—by the time Andrew Jackson was elected president in 1828, nearly all white men could vote—scrap-voting had become more or less a travesty, not least because the newest members of the electorate, poor men and immigrants, were the least likely to know how to write.[24]

In stepped political parties, whose rise to power was made possible by the rise of the paper ballot. Party leaders began to *print* ballots, usually in newspapers, either long strips, listing an entire slate, or pages meant to be cut to pieces, one for each candidate. These ballots came to be called "party tickets" because they looked like train tickets (and which is why, when we talk about someone who votes a single-party slate, we say that he "votes the party ticket"). The printing on ballots of party symbols (that's where the elephant and the donkey come from) meant that voters not only didn't need to know how to write; they didn't need to know how to read, either.[25]

At first, party tickets looked to be illegal. In 1829, a Boston man named David Henshaw tried to cast as his ballot a sheet of paper on which were printed the names of fifty-five candidates, his party's entire slate. Election officials refused to accept his ballot. Henshaw sued, arguing that he had been disenfranchised. When the case was heard before the state's supreme court, the decision turned on whether casting a printed ballot violated a clause in the state's constitution, requiring a written one. The Massachusetts Constitution, only decades old, had already been outpaced by the times. "It probably did not occur to the framers of the constitution," the Court observed, in a landmark ruling in Henshaw's favor, "that many of the towns might become so populous as to make it convenient to use printed votes."[26]

The ticket system made voting easier but only at the cost of limiting voters' choices. It also consolidated the power of the major parties while, curiously, promoting insurgency, too: party malcontents could print their own ballots, promoting their own slate of candidates; "knife" a candidate by stacking up a pile of tickets and then slicing out someone's name from the whole stack at once; or distribute "pasters," strips of paper with the name of a candidate not on the party ticket, to be pasted over his opponent's name. (Polls were stocked with vats of paste.)[27] Party tickets led to massive fraud, corruption, and intimidation. A candidate had to pay party leaders a hefty sum to ensure that his name would appear on the ticket and to cover the costs of printing tickets and buying votes. (One estimate put the midcentury price of a congressional seat in New York City at over $200,000.)[28] Ballots grew bigger and more colorful, so brightly colored that there was no way a voter could hide his vote.

But wanting to hide that vote now began to seem, in some quarters, eminently reasonable.[29] In 1851, the Massachusetts legislature mandated the use of uniform envelopes, to be supplied by the secretary of state. This proved controversial. "To say that the citizen shall vote with a sealed bag, or not at all," critics argued, "is an act of despotism." What honest man was ashamed of his vote?[30] In 1853, when the Massachusetts legislature changed hands, the new majority made envelopes optional, having accepted the argument that it was its duty to give every citizen the right "to vote as his fathers, did, with an open ballot."[31]

Meanwhile, on the other side of the world, someone came up with a startling idea. What if the government were to provide not just envelopes but ballots, too? An election law passed in Australia in 1856 detailed, quite minutely, the conduct of elections, ordering that no campaigning could take place within a certain distance of the polls and requiring that election officials print ballots and erect a booth or hire rooms, to be divided into compartments where voters could mark those ballots secretly. In 1888, Massachusetts passed An Act to Provide for Printing and Distributing Ballots, the model for all that followed.[32] Elsewhere, state legislatures swiftly adopted the same reform, persuaded, no doubt, of the need to clean up elections but also, in some places, eager to solve the "problem" of the expansion of the suffrage by . . . restricting it.

An Australian ballot, a ballot printed by the government, a ballot that voters had, even minimally, to *read*, made it much harder for immigrants, former slaves, and the uneducated poor to vote. (Women, of course, couldn't vote until the passage of the Nineteenth Amendment, in 1920.) Some precincts formally imposed and selectively administered literacy tests; others resorted to ranker chicanery (in 1894, one Virginian congressional district printed its ballots in Gothic letters). In the South, where black men had been granted suffrage by the Reconstruction Act of 1867, it was fear of the

black, Republican majority that led many former Confeder-
ate states to adopt the reform in the first place. As a Democratic campaign song sung in Arkansas in 1893 put it:

> The Australian ballot works like a charm
> It makes them think and scratch
> And when a Negro gets a ballot
> He has certainly met his match.

The year after Arkansas passed its Australian ballot law, the
percentage of black men who managed to vote dropped from
71 to 38.[33] That wasn't remedied until 1965, with the passage
of the Voting Rights Act.

Times change. That's why everyone can vote. And that's
why we're not still voting with corn and beans.

At the Green Dragon Tavern, I asked Austin Hess whether
he was worried Sarah Palin was hijacking the Tea Party. He
shrugged. "The enemy of my enemy is my friend," he said.
"I don't agree with her about a whole lot of things, but we're
not conducting purity tests. We're building coalitions." Patrick Humphries came by, handing out flyers about Tax Day.
Humphries didn't have much use for Palin, either. "She's
flamboyant. She's matured a lot. She has the right mind-set,
but she's not our leader. We don't need a leader. We're all
about devolution. We're going back to the Constitution. If
she were running for president, would I vote for her? Eh."

Humphries was born in Indiana and grew up in Iowa.
"I have always been a conservative," he told me, taking a
seat. "I register Republican once a year, for the primaries,
and then reregister as an Independent. I was not a supporter
of McCain, who wasn't a true conservative." He went to his
first Tea Party meeting in March 2009. "The radical change

that is going on has to be stopped. The losses of liberty are startling. I don't think people understand the government takeover of the economy, but it will represent a loss of freedom." Humphries and I kept talking past one another. He started talking about the Louisiana Purchase. I thought he meant Jefferson's deal with Napoleon, in 1803. No, he meant the payoff of $300 million in federal money to the state of Louisiana to buy Democratic senator Mary Landrieu's support for the health care plan.

Humphries didn't vote for Barack Obama; he didn't like what he was doing; he didn't want to foot anyone else's bills; he sent Scott Brown to Washington to stop all that, and Nancy Pelosi thwarted him. Humphries was concerned about his liberty. He handed me a pocket-sized copy of the Constitution, printed by the National Center for Constitutional Studies, whose website refers to the Constitution as a "miracle" and also sells a biography series called "The Real Founding Fathers," as endorsed by Glenn Beck. "I don't think the Founding Fathers wanted lobbyists running around Washington," Humphries said. He quoted the Tenth Amendment: "The powers not delegated to the United States by the Constitution, nor prohibited by it to the States, are reserved to the States respectively, or to the people." Humphries felt both powerless and poorly represented and even disenfranchised; he wanted that power he was supposed to get from the Tenth Amendment. "The Constitution gave us a bedrock. Ours was meant to be a very simple, straightforward government. The more power and money that goes to Washington, the less that's available to the states and to the people."

The National Center for Constitutional Studies was started in Utah in 1967, to promote originalism, the idea that the original intent of the framers is knowable and fixed and the final word. When the framers were still alive, people who wanted to know what they meant, by, say, a particular phrase, couldn't really ask them. Delegates to the Constitutional Convention pledged themselves to secrecy. And the more time passed, the remoter the Revolution, the more inscrutable the documents (even the meaning of the *words* changed), the greater the distance between now and then, the more demanding the act of interpretation. In 1816, when Jefferson was seventy-three, many of his Revolutionary generation having already died, he offered this answer, when asked what the framers would suggest about how to deal with this problem. "This they would say themselves, were they to rise from the dead": "laws and institutions must go hand in hand with the progress of the human mind." (To paraphrase the historian Carl Becker, the question the Enlightenment asked was not, "What would our forefathers do?" but "How can we make society better?")[34] Jefferson put it this way: "Some men look at constitutions with sanctimonious reverence, and deem them like the ark of the covenant, too sacred to be touched. They ascribe to the men of the preceding age a wisdom more than human." In Federalist 14, Madison asked, "Is it not the glory of the people of America, that, whilst they have paid a decent regard to the opinions of former times and other nations, they have not suffered a blind veneration for antiquity, for custom, or for names, to overrule the suggestions of their own good sense, the knowledge of their own situation, and the lessons of their own experience?"[35] The founders were not prophets. Nor did they hope to be worshipped. They believed that to defer without examination to what your forefathers believed is to become a slave to the tyranny of the past.

Nowhere has the tyranny of the past proven more despotic than on the matters having to do with race. In the decades between the Revolution and the Civil War, every story about the Revolution was a story about slavery, and the Constitution's failure to end it. "The page of impartial history bears testimony to the fact that the first martyr in the American Revolution was a colored man by the name of Attucks, who fell in King street, Boston," a Boston-born African American abolitionist named William Cooper Nell pointed out in 1848, launching a campaign to erect a statue to Attucks on the Common. (Nell is the historian who found that runaway slave ad, from 1750, identifying Crispus Attucks as a fugitive from Framingham.) The next year, in *Mardi*, Herman Melville's narrator travels to a fictionalized republic, where hieroglyphics chiseled in an arch at the entrance read: "In-this-republi-can-land-all-men-are-born-free-and-equal" but then, in smaller letters, "Except-the-tribe-of-Hamo."[36] That same year, Boston's blacks petitioned the school committee to integrate the city's public schools, insisting on racial equality.[37] In 1850, in *Roberts v. City of Boston*, Lemuel Shaw, chief justice of the Massachusetts Supreme Judicial Court (and Melville's father-in-law), upheld segregation, countering Charles Sumner's claim that segregation was based on nothing more than prejudice by declaring, "This prejudice is not created by law, and probably cannot be changed by law." (Shaw's ruling was later cited in *Plessy v. Ferguson*.) In Massachusetts, the first test of the 1850 Fugitive Slave Act came the next year, when Shaw heard the case of Thomas Sims. Shaw ruled that the fugitive Sims must be returned to slavery. "What a moment was lost," Emerson wrote, "when Judge Shaw declined to affirm the unconstitutionality of the Fugitive Slave Law!" Meanwhile, Nell petitioned the Massachusetts legislature for funding for his Attucks statue. After the legislature said no, in 1851, Nell led black Bostonians in celebrating Crispus Attucks Day, every fifth of March, in Faneuil Hall.[38] When Theodore Parker gave an address in Boston in 1852, on the first anniversary of Sims's being taken back into slavery, he insisted that Bostonians had no right to celebrate the Revolution so long as slavery endured. "Some of you, I think, keep trophies from that day, won at Concord or at Lexington," Parker said. "I have seen such things,—powderhorns, shoe-buckles, and other things from the nineteenth of April 1775. Here is a Boston trophy from April 19, 1851. This is the coat of Thomas Sims." He held up a garment, ripped to tatters. "Go Massachusetts! keep thy trophies from Lexington! I will keep this coat to remind me of Boston, and her dark places, which are full of cruelty."[39] On July 4, 1854, William Lloyd Garrison spoke at an antislavery rally in Framingham. Standing in front of an American flag hung upside down and bordered in black, Garrison burned a copy of the Constitution, calling it a "covenant with death, an agreement with hell." As the crowd cried, "Amen," Garrison ground the ashes of the Constitution beneath the heel of his shoe.[40]

That same year, Anthony Burns, who was born into slavery in Virginia, stowed away aboard a ship heading for Boston, explaining, "I heard of a North where men of my color could live without any man daring to say to them, 'You are my property.'"[41] In Boston, Burns was arrested under the terms of the Fugitive Slave Act. Boston's Vigilance Committee protested his arrest at Faneuil Hall on May 26. Thomas Wentworth Higginson left the meeting and, with a crowd of like-minded men, went to the Court House, to try to rescue Burns. In the melee, a federal marshal was killed. Later, when marshals marched Burns to the docks, there to board a boat to Virginia, fifty thousand Bostonians marched alongside, crying out, "Kidnappers!"[42] In 1855, when William Cooper

Nell published *Colored Patriots of the American Revolution*, Harriet Beecher Stowe supplied an introduction, noting that black patriots had rendered magnanimous service, fighting for "a nation which did not acknowledge them as citizens and equals." The book's frontispiece is an engraving of the Boston Massacre, based on Paul Revere's, in which Attucks has collapsed into the arms of white patriots. In the foreground, fallen from his head, lies his tricornered hat.[43] In antebellum America, every story about the Revolution was a story about slavery.

In 1857, in *Dred Scott v. Sandford*, the Supreme Court, enslaved to the tyranny of the past, ruled that the framers had considered blacks "as beings of an inferior order, and altogether unfit to associate with the white race, either in social or political relations; and so far inferior, that they have no rights which the white man was bound to respect."[44] That's what Illinois senator Stephen Douglas and his Republican challenger, Abraham Lincoln, debated, the next year. "I believe that this government was made on the white basis," Douglas said. "It was made by white men for the benefit of white men and their posterity forever." Lincoln disagreed: "I believe the entire records of the world, from the date of the Declaration of Independence up to within three years ago, may be searched in vain for one single affirmation, from one single man, that the negro was not included in the Declaration of Independence," he said. "I think I may defy Douglas to show that any President ever said so—that any member of Congress ever said so—or that any man ever said so, until the necessities of the Democratic party had to invent that."[45]

The question debated by Lincoln and Douglas was historical, but the founding documents couldn't settle it because the founders hadn't settled it. Even the Civil War didn't settle it.

"Have You Ever Seen the Words Forced Busing in the Constitution?" That was a sign carried in Boston, on March 5, 1975, at a reenactment of the Boston Massacre on its 205th anniversary. In 1974, Judge W. Arthur Garrity, a federal district court judge, mandated the integration of Boston's public schools—requiring the forced busing of children, from one neighborhood to another. White antibusing activists turned up at Bicentennial events in force. As J. Anthony Lukas reported in *Common Ground*, "Opponents of busing saw themselves as victims of the same oppression which had beset eighteenth-century Bostonians and said they were fighting for the same right to control their own lives. State Representative Ray Flynn warned, 'The sacred principles on which this nation was founded are threatened by a new tyranny, a tyranny dressed in judicial robes.'" On the day of the 1975 Boston Massacre reenactment, four hundred antibusing protesters in colonial garb marched to the Old State House carrying a coffin marked "R.I.P. Liberty, Born 1770—Died 1974." When the reenactors portraying Preston's grenadiers fired, all four hundred protesters fell to the ground.[46]

Just weeks later, on April 18, 1975, the two hundredth anniversary of Paul Revere's ride, Gerald Ford came to Boston. Nixon had abolished the American Bicentennial Commission in 1973, replacing it with the American Revolution Bicentennial Administration. In August of that year, Nixon had resigned; Ford pardoned him in September. Now, in a speech at the Old North Church, Ford called on Americans to learn, by examining their history, that "the American experience has been more of reason than revolution." Across town, at the annual meeting of the Organization of American Historians, Arthur Schleslinger Jr. spoke about his new book, *The Imperial Presidency*.[47] In Concord, thirty thousand protesters, under the banner of the Peoples Bicentennial Commission, were camping out, while Pete Seeger and Arlo Guthrie played through the night. Rifkin said, "The theme of the demonstration is 'Send a Message to Wall Street,' and we want the corporations to know, by our mass presence at Concord, that people are fed up with them running the country."[48] By morning, over a hundred thousand people had gathered in Concord, awaiting the president.

Meanwhile, the evacuation of Saigon was beginning. Ford had already authorized early airlifts. At ten o'clock on the morning of April 19, 1975, Ford arrived in Concord, by helicopter. In the two centuries since the shot heard round the world, the president said, "The United States has become a world power." He boasted of American military might, decried isolationism, acknowledged the past, and argued for change, quoting Jefferson: "Nothing then is unchangeable but the inherent and inalienable rights of man." He said he hoped that, at the Tricentennial, in a hundred years, people would look back at this day and see it as the first in a century of American unity. After Ford flew away and the protesters went home, one *Globe* reporter wrote, all that was left was trash, and a sign reading "The Revolution is Not Over."[49] Saigon fell eleven days later.

Two months later, on June 17, 1975, during a two hundredth anniversary reenactment of the Battle of Bunker Hill conducted by the Charlestown Militia, someone hung an antibusing banner from a window of a house alongside Monument Square. It read, "We're right back where we began 200 years ago."[50]

Originalism as a school of constitutional interpretation has waxed and waned and has always competed with other schools of interpretation. Madison's invaluable notes on the Constitutional Convention weren't published until 1840, and nineteenth-century constitutional theory differed, dramatically, from the debates that have taken place in the twentieth century. In the 1950s and 1960s, the Supreme Court rejected originalist arguments put forward by southern segregationists, stating, in *Brown v. Board of Education* in 1954, that "we cannot turn back the clock" but "must consider public education in the light of its full development and its present place in American life throughout the Nation." Constitutional scholars generally date the rise of originalism to the 1970s and consider it a response to controversial decisions of both the Warren and Burger Courts, especially *Roe v. Wade*, in 1973. Originalism received a great deal of attention in 1987, with the Supreme Court nomination of Robert Bork.[51] Bork's nomination also happened to coincide with the bicentennial of the Constitutional Convention. "Nineteen eighty-seven marks the 200th anniversary of the United States Constitution," Thurgood Marshall said in a speech that year. Marshall (who went to Frederick Douglass High School) had argued *Brown v. Board of Education* in 1954 and, in 1967, after being nominated by Lyndon Johnson, became the first African American on the Supreme Court. In 1987, contemplating the bicentennial of the Constitution, Marshall took a skeptical view.

The focus of this celebration invites a complacent belief that the vision of those who debated and compromised in Philadelphia yielded the "more perfect Union" it is said we now enjoy. I cannot accept this invitation, for I do not believe that the meaning of the Constitution was forever "fixed" at the Philadelphia Convention. Nor do I find the wisdom, foresight, and sense of justice exhibited by the Framers particularly profound. To the contrary, the government they devised was defective from the start, requiring several amendments, a civil war, and major social transformations to attain the system of constitutional government and its respect for the freedoms and individual rights, we hold as fundamental today.

Marshall was worried about what anniversaries do. "The odds are that for many Americans the bicentennial celebration will be little more than a blind pilgrimage to the shrine of the original document now stored in a vault in the National Archives," rather than the occasion for "a sensitive understanding of the Constitution's inherent defects, and its promising evolution through 200 years of history." Expressing doubts about unthinking reverence, Marshall called for something different:

> In this bicentennial year, we may not all participate in the festivities with flagwaving fervor. Some may more quietly commemorate the suffering, struggle, and sacrifice that has triumphed over much of what was wrong with the original document, and observe the anniversary with hopes not realized and promises not fulfilled. I plan to celebrate the bicentennial of the Constitution as a living document.[52]

Even as Marshall was making that speech, the banner of originalism was being taken up by evangelicals, who, since joining the Reagan Revolution in 1980, had been playing an increasingly prominent role in American politics. "Any diligent student of American history finds that our great nation was founded by godly men upon godly principles to be a Christian nation," Jerry Falwell insisted. In 1987, Tim La-Haye, an evangelical minister who went on to write a series of best-selling apocalyptic novels, published a book called *The Faith of Our Founding Fathers*, in which he attempted to chronicle the "Rape of History" by "history revisionists" who had systemically erased from American textbooks the "evangelical Protestants who founded this nation." Documenting this claim was no mean feat. Jefferson posed a particular problem, not least because he crafted a custom copy of the Bible by cutting out all the miracles and pasting together what was left. LaHaye, to support his argument, took out his own pair of scissors, deciding, for instance, that Jefferson didn't count as a Founding Father because he "had nothing to do with the founding of our nation," and basing his claims about Benjamin Franklin not on evidence (because, as he admitted, "There is no evidence that Franklin ever became a Christian"), but on sheer bald, raising-the-founders-from-the-dead assertion. LaHaye wrote, "Many modern secularizers try to claim Franklin as one of their own. I am confident, however, that Franklin would not identify with them were he alive today."[53] (Alas, Franklin, who once said he wished he could preserve himself in a vat of Madeira wine, to see what the world would look like in a century or two, is not, in fact, alive today.[54] And, while I confess that I'm quite excessively fond of him, the man is not coming back.)

Lincoln was a lawyer, Douglas a judge; they had studied the law; they disagreed about how to interpret the founding documents, but they also shared a set of ideas about standards of evidence and the art of rhetoric, which is why they were able to hold, over seven days, such a substantial and relentless debate. Falwell and LaHaye were evangelical ministers; what they shared was the art of extracting passages from scripture and using them to preach a gospel about good and bad, heaven and hell, damnation and salvation.

"My faith is the faith of my fathers," Mitt Romney declared in an address on faith, in 2007, just before the presidential primary season, during which Romney sought the Republican nomination. Romney's Founding Fathers weren't the usual ones, though. Historians of religious liberty have typically referred to four foundational texts: Madison's 1785 "Memorial Remonstrance against Religious Assessments" ("The Religion of every man must be left to the conviction and conscience of every man"), a statute written by Jefferson ("our civil rights have no dependence on our religious opinions any more than our opinions in physics or geometry"), Article VI of the Constitution ("no religious test shall ever be required as a qualification to any office or public trust under the United States"), and the First Amendment ("Congress shall make no law respecting an establishment of religion, or prohibiting the free exercise thereof"). Romney, though, skipped over Jefferson and Madison in favor of Brigham Young, John and Samuel Adams, and the seventeenth-century Puritan dissenter, Roger Williams, in order to accuse modern-day secularists of being "at odds with the nation's founders," and of having taken the doctrine of separation of church and state "well beyond its original meaning" by seeking "to remove from the public domain any acknowledgement of God."[55]

Precisely what the founders believed about God, Jesus, sin, the Bible, churches, and hell is probably impossible to discover. They changed their minds and gave different accounts to different people: Franklin said one thing to his sister, Jane, and another thing to David Hume; Washington prayed with his troops, but, while he lay slowly dying, he declined to call for a preacher. This can make them look like hypocrites, but that's unfair, as are a great many attacks on these men. They approached religion more or less the same way they approached everything else that interested them: Franklin invented his own, Washington proved diplomatic, Adams grumbled about it (he hated Christianity, he once said, but he couldn't think of anything better, and he also regarded it as necessary), Jefferson could not stop tinkering with it, and Madison defended, as a natural right, the free exercise of it. That they wanted to preserve religious liberty by separating church and state does not mean they were irreligious. They wanted to protect religion from the state, as much as the other way around.

Nevertheless, if the founders had followed their forefathers, they would have written a Constitution establishing Christianity as the national religion. Nearly every British North American colony was settled with an established religion; Connecticut's 1639 charter explained that the whole purpose of government was "to mayntayne and presearve the liberty and purity of the gospel of our Lord Jesus." In the century and a half between the Connecticut charter and the 1787 meeting of the Constitutional Convention lies an entire revolution, not just a political revolution but also a religious revolution. Following the faith of their fathers is exactly what the framers did not do. At a time when all but two states required religious tests for office, the Constitution prohibited them. At a time when all but three states still had an official religion, the Bill of Rights forbade the federal government from establishing one.[56]

Originalism in the courts is controversial, to say the least. Jurisprudence stands on precedent, on the stability of the laws, but originalism is hardly the only way to abide by the Constitution. Setting aside the question of whether it makes good law, it is, generally, lousy history. And it has long since reached well beyond the courts. Set loose in the culture, and tangled together with fanaticism, originalism looks like history, but it's not; it's historical fundamentalism, which is to history what astrology is to astronomy, what alchemy is to chemistry, what creationism is to evolution.

In eighteenth-century America, I wouldn't have been able to vote. I wouldn't have been able to own property, either. I'd very likely have been unable to write, and, if I survived childhood, chances are that I'd have died in childbirth. And, no matter how long or short my life, I'd almost certainly have died without having once ventured a political opinion preserved in any historical record, except that none of these factors has any meaning or bearing whatsoever on whether an imaginary eighteenth-century me would have supported the Obama administration's stimulus package or laws allowing the carrying of concealed weapons or the war in Iraq, because I did not live in eighteenth-century America, and no amount of thinking that I could, not even wearing petticoats, a linsey-woolsey calico smock, and a homespun mobcap, can make it so. Citizens and their elected officials have all sorts of reasons to support or oppose all sorts of legislation and government action, including constitutionality, precedence, and the weight of history. But it's possible to cherish the stability of the law and the durability of the Constitution, as amended over two and a half centuries of change and one civil war, and tested in the courts, without dragging the Founding Fathers from their graves. To point this out neither dishonors the past nor relieves anyone of the obligation to study it. To the contrary.

"What would the founders do?" is, from the point of view of historical analysis, an ill-considered and unanswerable question, and pointless, too. Jurists and legislators need to investigate what the framers meant, and some Christians make moral decisions by wondering what Jesus would do, but no NASA scientist decides what to do about the Hubble by asking what Isaac Newton would make of it. People who ask what the founders would do quite commonly declare that they know, they know, they just know what the founders would do and, mostly, it comes to this: if only they could see us now, they would be rolling over in their graves. They might even rise from the dead and walk among us. We have failed to obey their sacred texts, holy writ. They suffered for us, and we have forsaken them. Come the Day of Judgment, they will damn us.

That's not history. It's not civil religion, the faith in democracy that binds Americans together. It's not originalism or even constitutionalism. That's fundamentalism.

CHAPTER 5

Your Superexcellent Age

Boston Common was lined with vendors the day the Tea Party Express drove into town, on April 14, 2010. You could buy: "Fox News Fan" T-shirts; "Tea Party Tea"; "Don't Tread on Me" flags; "Straight Pride" signs; a pin that read

Spell-Check
says
OBAMA is
OSAMA;

a tote bag picturing a revolver and the caption "An Armed Society Is a Polite Society"; and, at a special day-of-the-rally discount, a copy of "The Constitution Made Easy." Christen Varley's Coalition for Marriage staffed a table. George and John Egan and Patrick Humphries were passing out Boston Tea Party information at two different tents. Scott Brown hadn't come; the Senate was in session. Charlie Baker, a Massachusetts Republican gubernatorial candidate who had breakfasted with the Boston Tea Party over the weekend, hadn't turned up, either. This was Sarah Palin's party.

Clustering around the bandstand, Cape Ann Tea Partiers jostled with Plymouth Rock Tea Partiers, every fourth hand carrying an American flag. A man in a hard hat, trying to make his way closer to stage, parted the waters by crying out, "The liberals are coming! The liberals are coming!" The Tea Party Express put on a musical show: "The Stars and Stripes Forever," "The Star-Spangled Banner," "America the Beautiful," "The Battle Hymn of the Republic." In between numbers, the crowd broke out into chanting, "USA! USA! USA!" Someone on the stage cried out, "I heard there ain't no party like a Boston Tea Party!"

Next came a call to recite the Pledge of Allegiance.

"I pledge allegiance to the flag—"

The original pledge was written by Francis Bellamy, the former pastor of Boston's Bethany Baptist Church. Bellamy, a socialist, was the vice president of the Society of Christian Socialists; his sermons and lectures included "Jesus the Socialist" and "Socialism and the Bible." He was also the cousin of Edward Bellamy, whose 1888 novel, *Looking Backward, 2000–1887*, imagined a man born in Boston in 1857 falling asleep in 1887 and waking up in the year 2000, to find a socialist utopia, a city with no more poor, with a public square—a Boston Common—on every corner, "open squares filled with trees, among which statues glistened and fountains flashed."

"—and to the Republic, for which it stands—"

Francis Bellamy wrote the Pledge of Allegiance for children, to recite at school; it wasn't meant for grown-ups. It was published in a Boston children's magazine, the *Youth's*

Companion, in 1892, on the occasion of the four hundredth anniversary of Columbus's discovery of America.

"—one nation—"

It became the national pledge in 1942.

"—under God—"

"Under God" was added in the 1950s.

"—indivisible—"

In the 1970s, white antibusing activists in Boston recited an antipledge: "We will not pledge allegiance to the order of the United States District Court, nor the dictatorship for which it stands; one order, under Garrity, with liberty and justice for none."

"—with liberty and justice—"

At a meeting in Boston in 1976, a group calling itself the Bicentennial Ethnic Racial Forum drafted a new pledge, swearing allegiance to "one nation of many people, cultures, languages, and colors." That went nowhere. The next year, Massachusetts governor Michael Dukakis vetoed a law requiring teachers to lead schoolchildren in daily recitations of the pledge. His veto became a partisan weapon during the presidential campaign of 1988, the campaign in which "liberal" became a smear. "What is it about the pledge that upsets him so much?" then vice president George Bush asked at a rally, in a particularly effective attack on his "card-carrying member of the ACLU" opponent.[1]

"—for all."

"Isn't this sweet?" said a woman standing next to me, smiling. She didn't wait for an answer. "I'm here to see Sarah. She's so adorable."

I took out my notebook. She frowned.

"Are you a liberal?" she asked, her voice rising.

"I'm a hist—"

"—because give me fifty bucks." She grabbed my jacket and yanked, hard. "Give me fifty bucks!"

"Fifty bucks?"

"If you're a liberal. Because you people, you want to give money to anyone who asks you."

In the winter of 1776, John Adams read *Common Sense*, an anonymous, radical, and brilliant forty-six-page pamphlet that would convince the American people of what more than a decade of taxes and nearly a year of war had not: that this battle wasn't just Boston's fight, and what's more, it wasn't even only America's fight. "The cause of America is in a great measure the cause of all mankind," was *Common Sense*'s astonishing and inspiring claim about the fate of thirteen infant colonies on the edge of the world. "The sun never shone on a cause of greater worth. 'Tis not the affair of a city, a county, a province, or a kingdom; but of a continent—of at least one-eighth part of the habitable globe. 'Tis not the concern of a day, a year, or an age; posterity are virtually involved in the contest, and will be more or less affected even to the end of time, by the proceedings now."[2] Everyone wondered: who could have written such stirring stuff? "People Speak of it in rapturous praise," a friend wrote Adams. "Some make Dr. Franklin the Author," hinted another. "I think I see strong marks of your pen in it," speculated a third. More miffed than flattered, Adams admitted to his wife, Abigail, "I could not have written any Thing in so manly and striking a style." Who, then? Adams found out: "His Name is Paine."[3]

"I offer nothing more than simple facts, plain arguments, and common sense," Paine wrote, but this was coyness itself: *Common Sense* stood every argument against American independence on its head. "There is something absurd in supposing a continent to be perpetually governed by an island," he insisted. He wanted Americans to grow up. As to the colonies' dependence on England, "We may as well assert that because a child has thrived upon milk, that it is never to have meat."[4] "He is a keen Writer," Adams allowed, but he had written only "a tolerable summary of the argument which I had been repeating again and again in Congress for nine months."[5]

George Washington, meanwhile, remained at his headquarters in Cambridge. (He lived in a house that Henry Wadsworth Longfellow would one day occupy.) Phillis Wheatley wrote to Washington that October, sending him a poem she had written about him, and signing off, "Wishing your Excellency all possible success in the great cause you are so generously engaged in." (Washington wrote back, graciously thanking her for the poem and inviting her to visit: "If you should ever come to Cambridge, or near headquarters, I shall be happy to see a person so favored by the Muses.")[6] The British and the Americans had been in a stalemate for months, but in November of 1775, Washington sent Knox, who had left bookselling behind in Boston, to bring back artillery captured from the British at Ticonderoga. When Knox turned up with sixty tons of artillery, in February of 1776, the Continentals fortified Dorchester Heights and, on March 2, began bombing the city. Two months after *Common Sense* was published, the Continental army blasted the British out of Boston and ended the siege. On March 17, the British evacuated. Eleven thousand people, more than nine thousand of them soldiers, sailed out of Boston Harbor. (The seventeenth of March, Evacuation Day, is a somewhat woebegotten public holiday in Boston; most people think schools and offices are closed, that day, because it happens, also, to be St. Patrick's Day.)

The city was in ruins. Before the British left, they took what they could and destroyed what they couldn't carry. Soldiers broke into Jane Mecom's house and plundered its contents.[7] "Such conduct would disgrace barbarians," Andrew Eliot wrote. "I am quite sick of Armies." But taking Boston back, Eliot thought, had changed the colonists' point of view entirely. "They look upon it as a complete victory." It had even changed Eliot's position. "I dare now to say what I did not dare to say before this—I have long thought it—that Great Britain *cannot* subjugate the colonies. Independence, a year ago, could not have been publicly mentioned with impunity. Nothing else is now talked of, and I know not what can be done by Great Britain to prevent it."[8]

In Philadelphia, the Continental Congress set about declaring independence. John Adams, Thomas Jefferson, Benjamin Franklin, Robert Livingston, and Roger Sherman served on a committee charged with drafting a declaration. At the time, Franklin had, as usual, much other business to attend to. Among other things, he was trying to find a place for his now violently deranged nephew, Benjamin Mecom, in Pennsylvania Hospital, America's first hospital, which Franklin had helped to found, in 1751, "to care for the sick poor of the Province and for the reception and care of lunaticks." There wasn't any room. In haste, Franklin arranged for Mecom to be confined in Burlington, New Jersey.[9]

Jefferson drafted the declaration. "When in the course of human Events, it becomes necessary for one People to dissolve the Political Bands which have connected them with another, and to assume among the Powers of the Earth, the separate and equal Station to which the Laws of Nature and of Nature's God entitle them, a decent Respect to the Opinions of Mankind requires that they should declare the causes which impel them to the Separation." Most of the declaration is a list of grievances, evidence of the British government's conspiracy against American liberties: "a long Train of Abuses and Usurpations, pursuing invariably the same Object, evinces a Design to reduce them under absolute Despotism." (Independence—rebellion—was extraordinary, a last resort. It required an elaborate justification, abuses compiled, compounded, over years and years.) Last on Jefferson's list, in his original draft, was slavery. In a breathless paragraph, his longest and angriest grievance against the king, Jefferson blamed George III for slavery ("He has waged cruel war against human nature itself, violating its most sacred rights of life and liberty in the persons of a distant people who never offended him, captivating and carrying them into slavery"), for colonists' failure to abolish the slave trade ("determined to keep open a market where men should be bought and sold, he has prostituted his negative for suppressing every legislative attempt to prohibit or restrain this execrable commerce"), and for Dunmore's Proclamation ("he is now exciting those very people to rise in arms among us, and to purchase that liberty of which he had deprived them, by murdering the people upon whom he also obtruded them: thus paying off former crimes committed against the liberties of one people, with crimes which he urges them to commit against the lives of another"). Jefferson's fellow delegates could not abide it. To some, it went too far; to others, it didn't go half far enough. And as everyone knew, it was they, and not the British, who were most vulnerable to charges of hypocrisy. They struck it out almost entirely; all that's left is "he has excited domestic insurrections among us" (which Franklin wrote). Abigail Adams complained to John: "I cannot but feel sorry that some of the most manly sentiments in the declaration are expunged."[10]

On July 14, 1776, the Declaration of Independence was read aloud in Boston, from the second floor balcony of the Town House. "A great Concourse of People assembled for the Occasion," a newspaper reported. The reading "was received with great Joy, expressed by three Huzzas." Canons were fired from forts surrounding the city. Church bells were rung. And then, later that night: "The King's Arms, and every sign with any Resemblance of it, whether Lion and Crown, Pestle and Mortar and Crown, Heart, and Crown &c. together with every Sign that belonged to a Tory was taken down, and the latter made a general Conflagration in King-Street." Inside the Council Chamber where James Otis had once argued the writs of assistance case, toasts were given, including one to "the downfall of Tyrants and Tyranny" and another to "the universal Prevalence of Civil and Religious Liberty."[11] That summer, Harry Washington, one of George Washington's slaves, left Mount Vernon and declared his own independence by running away to fight with Dunmore's "Ethiopian Regiment," wearing, some said, a uniform bearing the motto "Liberty to Slaves."[12]

"Everybody talked about the Bicentennial," Russell Baker wrote in the *New York Times* on New Year's Day 1976, "but nobody did anything about it." Irked, John Warner, former secretary of the navy and the chairman of the American Revolution Bicentennial Administration, wrote a reply. The Bicentennial, he explained, was to "honor the great men who forged and then steered a nation so strong and so flexible that one revolution has proved enough."[13] Nevertheless, the Bicentennial was beleaguered. On March 17, 1976, the two hundredth anniversary of the evacuation of Boston, a subcommittee of the Senate Judiciary Committee convened hearings into "The

Attempt to Steal the Bicentennial" by the Peoples Bicentennial Commission. Mississippi senator James Eastland chaired the investigation. Eastland had been one of the South's most ardent segregationists. Commenting on *Brown v. Board of Education*, he had said, "On May 17, 1954, the Constitution of the United States was destroyed because of the Supreme Court's decision," and had told his constituents, "There is no law that a free people must submit to a flagrant invasion of their personal liberty."[14] In 1964, when three civil rights workers were killed in Mississippi, Eastland told Lyndon Johnson, "I believe it was a publicity stunt." ("Jim Eastland could be standing right in the middle of the worst Mississippi flood ever known," Johnson once said, "and he'd say the niggers caused it, helped out by the communists.")[15] Eastland's committee heard testimony that Rifkin's commission had managed to get more and better press coverage than the federal government's own commission. Eastland said he wanted to "peel back the patriotic veneer" of the Peoples Bicentennial Commission. But the hearings ended, inconclusively, after only two days.[16]

Ford, meanwhile, was taking a different approach to the Bicentennial than Nixon had. His appointments to the American Revolution Bicentennial Administration included Alex Haley, Malcolm X's ghostwriter, and Betty Shabazz, Malcolm X's widow. The highlight of the Bicentennial, across the nation, came on July 4, 1976, the nation's birthday. Everywhere there were fireworks, parades, concerts. There was a seventy-six-hour vigil at the National Archives. Walter Cronkite called it "the greatest, most colossal birthday party in 200 years." An editorial in the *Washington Post* spoke of a national reconciliation, a renewed patriotism: "Now the flag is common property again, to be stapled onto parade floats, stuck in hats and hung from front porches."[17] Boston celebrated with a concert on the Charles, attended by four hundred thousand people, and fireworks that night. Still, it was hard to get past the coincidence of the city's antibusing riots and its bid for national attention during the Bicentennial. And what most people remember about that coincidence is a single picture, taken on April 5, 1976, at an antibusing demonstration outside Government Center, just across from Faneuil Hall, and printed on the front page of newspapers across the country: a Pulitzer Prize–winning black-and-white photograph of a white teenager attempting to impale a black man with the American flag.[18]

"Look, a BLACK Tea Partier," read the sign Kat Malone was carrying the day Sarah Palin came to Boston. Boston Common is either decorated with the city's history or scarred with it, depending on how you look at it. A memorial to Crispus Attucks was erected on Boston Common in 1888. Nine years later, farther up toward the State House, there followed a memorial to Robert Gould Shaw and the Fifty-fourth Regiment of Foot, the African American battalion Shaw commanded during the Civil War. Robert Lowell wrote a poem about it in 1960: "Their monument sticks like a fishbone / in the city's throat."[19] Now, steps from those monuments, Tea Partiers wore T-shirts that said

AMERICAN
NOT
RACIST

The flags waved. The speeches began. "Mr. Obama, we want the southern border shut down so tight a rattlesnake couldn't cross it," said John Philip Sousa IV, of the Tea Party Express. National talk-radio host and Tea Party Express chairman, Mark Williams, took the stage. "I'm home!" Williams shouted. "I am here to reclaim my hometown for America. The hippies have had it long enough." He attacked the lamestream media: "The *Globe* will read about this tomorrow in the *Herald*." He called for Barney Frank's resignation. He lambasted Harvard, communists in Cambridge, and communists in the White House. "Political correctness led to 9/11. Political correctness led to Barack Hussein Obama." The next time he mentioned the president, Williams didn't bother with his last name and called him, simply, "Barack Hussein." To some people in the Tea Party, Obama's administration, his very presidency, was unconstitutional; the man wasn't even an American.

Debbie Lee, whose son was the first Navy Seal to die in Iraq, told the story of her son's life and death. Our troops are fighting this war abroad, she said, and we are fighting it here on the home front. Taps was played. Standing where, in 1971, Vietnam Veterans Against the War, dressed in battle fatigues and carrying babies in backpacks, had listened to Eugene McCarthy tell them they were bearing witness to life and peace, the Tea Partiers grew hushed, and found redemption, in death and war.

Palin's warm-up, a musician named Lloyd Marcus, took the stage. "I am not an African American," he shouted. "I am Lloyd Marcus, an AMERICAN." He sang the "National Tea Party Anthem": "When they call you a racist because you disagree, that's another one of their nasty tricks." Then he broke out into revival-style call-and-response. "Are y'all racists?" he hollered out to the crowd. "No!" Here, at last, was absolution.

Austin Hess spent much of his time working hard to make sure clusters of protesters and counterprotesters didn't break out into fisticuffs. "Moonbats Go Back to Harvard" read one sign. (Howie Carr, a columnist for the *Boston Herald*, regularly calls liberals moonbats.) Caleb Waugh, a graduate student from MIT, was carrying a sign that read "Nucular Engineers for Palin!!1!" He said he was going for "a Steven Colbert approach." Nearby, a man from Beacon Hill carried a sign reading "Our Tea Party Is NOT Yours." Next to him, a Tea Partier waved a warning: "Moonbat ⇒."

The former governor of Alaska arrived. She grabbed hold of the microphone. "I love Boston," she said. It's "the town that the Sons of Liberty called home." She spoke of the city's history: "You're sounding the warning bell just like what happened in that midnight run and just like with that original tea party back in 1773." She talked about life in the United States: "Is that what Barack Obama meant, when he promised the nation that they would fundamentally transform America?" she asked. "Is this what their 'change' is all about? I want to tell him, 'Nah, you know, we, we'll keep clinging to our Constitution, and our guns, and religion, and you can keep the change.'"

In the far right, where originalism has slipped into fundamentalism, where historical scholarship is taken for a conspiracy and the founding of the United States has become a religion, it's not the past that's a foreign country. It's the present.

"These are the times that try men's souls," Thomas Paine wrote in December 1776, by the light of a campfire during Washington's desperate retreat across New Jersey. Paine donated his share of the profits from *Common Sense* to buy supplies for the Continental army, in which he also served, but his chief contribution to the war was a series of essays known as the *American Crisis*. Making ready to cross the frozen Delaware River—at night, in a blizzard—to launch a surprise attack on Trenton, Washington ordered Paine's words read to his exhausted, frostbitten troops: "The summer soldier and the sunshine patriot will, in this crisis, shrink from the service of their country; but he that stands it now, deserves the love and thanks of man and woman. Tyranny, like hell, is not easily conquered; yet we have this consolation with us, that the harder the conflict, the more glorious the triumph."[20] The next morning, the Continentals fought to a stunning victory.

While the war lasted, Benjamin Edes paid a fine for failing to serve in the army in order to print his *Gazette*. After the British evacuated Boston, Edes moved his printing press back to the city. Andrew Eliot, though, made plans to move to Concord, in case Boston should fall to the British once again. Eliot died in 1778; at his death, Edes's *Gazette* lamented that the reverend had gone "off the Stage of Action entirely unnoticed."[21] Benjamin Mecom escaped from the house in New Jersey where Benjamin Franklin had arranged for him to be confined. He disappeared during the Battle of Trenton and, as Jane Mecom wrote to her brother, had "never been heard of since."[22] The farmer's wife who was taking care of Jane Mecom's other mad son, Peter, asked for more money, five dollars a week, threatening that if she didn't get it, "she would send him to boston." This terrified Jane Mecom, who tried "to git Him Put in to the Alms house" but was told "there is no provision for such persons there." Peter Franklin Mecom died not long after, deprived of reason, deprived, even, of speech. As his mother wrote, he "sunk in to Eternity without a Groan."[23] Ralph Waldo Emerson's grandfather, William Emerson, enlisted in the Continental army, as a chaplain, but fell sick on the march to Ticonderoga and died in 1778.[24] That year, Phillis Wheatley returned to Boston, married a black shopkeeper named John Peters, and announced her plan to publish a second book of poems, to be dedicated to Benjamin Franklin. It was never published. Instead, she gave birth to three children in the space of five years. Her husband went to debtors' prison. Her first two children were dead by the time she gave birth to her third. She died, at the age of thirty-one, of childbed fever, along with the baby at her breast. "The world is a severe schoolmaster," Wheatley once wrote. She was buried, with her infant daughter, in an unmarked grave on Copp's Hill.[25]

During the war, tens of thousands of slaves left their homes, escaping from slavery to the freedom promised by the British, and betting on British victory. They lost that bet. They died in battle, they died of disease, they ended up someplace else, they ended up back where they started, and worse off. (A fifteen-year-old girl captured while heading for Dunmore's regiment was greeted by her master with a whipping of eighty lashes, after which he poured hot embers into her wounds.) When the British evacuated, thousands of blacks went with them, in port after port. In Charleston, after all the ships were full, British soldiers patrolled the wharves to keep back the flocks of black men, women, and children frantic to leave the United States rather than be taken back up into slavery. A handful managed to duck under the redcoats' raised bayonets, jump off the docks, and swim out to the last longboats ferrying passengers to the British fleet—whose crowded ships included the aptly named *Free Briton*. Clinging to the sides of the longboats, they were not allowed on board, but neither would they let go; in the end, their fingers were chopped off.[26]

Harry Washington, who had run away from Mount Vernon, left America in 1783. A clerk dutifully noted his departure in the "Book of Negroes," a handwritten ledger listing the three thousand runaway slaves and free blacks who evacuated from New York with the British that summer: "Harry Washington, 43, fine fellow. Formerly the property of General Washington; left him 7 years ago."[27] Washington, with some fifteen hundred families, settled in bleak Birchtown, Nova Scotia. By the time he arrived there in August of 1783, though, there was nothing to eat, it was too late to plant, and it turned out that the topsoil was too thin to plant much, anyway. Two years later, the settlers were still starving. A settler named Boston King reported, "Many of the poor people were compelled to sell their best gowns for five pounds of flour, in order to support life. When they had parted with all their clothes, even to their blankets, several of them fell down dead in the streets, thro' hunger. Some killed and ate their dogs and cats; and poverty and distress prevailed on every side." They made a plan to leave, and to sail to Sierra Leone. In January 1792, nearly twelve hundred black men, women, and children, including Harry Washington, found berths on fifteen ships in Halifax harbor. Each family received a certificate "indicating the plot of land 'free of expence' they were to be given 'upon arrival in Africa.'" But the colony's new capital, the Province of Freedom, did not live up to its name. Boston King's wife, Violet, died of "putrid fever" within weeks of arrival. The promised plots turned out to be not so free after all; investors demanded exorbitant quit rent payments. "We wance did call it Free Town," one worn-out settler wrote in 1795, but now "have a reason to call it a town of slavery." By 1799 Sierra Leone's settlers had become so discontent, so revolutionary in their rejection of the colony's white government, that it was said they were "as thorough Jacobins as if they had been trained and educated in Paris." The next year, a group of rebels tried to form a sovereign republic. They were crushed. Tried by a special military tribunal, they were banished from Freetown to the other side of the Sierra Leone River. In their exile, they elected Harry Washington as their leader, just months after George Washington died at Mount Vernon.[28]

In 1777, Vermont became the first state to outlaw slavery. That same year, John Adams defeated a bill put forward, in the Massachusetts legislature, to do the same.[29] Slavery ended in Massachusetts in the 1780s, with vague court rulings, reinforced by the weight of public opinion.[30] James Otis was killed by lightning in 1784. Sometime before he died, he burned all of his papers in a bonfire that lasted two days. In 1785, the government of Massachusetts passed its own stamp tax. Benjamin Edes argued against it, signing himself "The Printer's Friend." Thomas Paine left the United States for England in 1787. "Where liberty is, there is my country," Franklin once said, to which Paine replied, "Wherever liberty is not, there is my country." Franklin spent the last years of his life in Philadelphia. He died in 1790, at the age of eighty-four. In his will, he left one hundred pounds to the public schools of Boston. To his sister, Jane, he left the house in which she lived. "Who that Know & Love you," Jane Mecom wrote to her brother, just months before he died, "can Bare the thoughts of Serviving you in this Gloomy world."[31]

Twenty thousand mourners came to Franklin's funeral, but his fate, in the American imagination, is a dreary tale. "Early to Bed, and early to rise, makes a Man healthy, wealthy and wise," Franklin had written in "The Way to Wealth." "The sorrow that that maxim has cost me through my parents' experimenting on me with it, tongue cannot tell," Mark Twain once wrote. By the time Twain was writing, in 1870, Poor Richard's parody, the useless advice to a wayward nephew, was taken literally. Of the thrifty, frugal, prudent, sober, homey, quaint, sexless, humorless, and preachy Benjamin Franklin, the prophet of prosperity, Twain wrote, "He was a hard lot."[32] To his twee reputation, Franklin's breathtakingly vast, cosmopolitan, enlightened, revolutionary life seems to matter not at all. As Poor Richard once said, sometimes "Force shites upon Reason's back."[33]

"It is an age of revolutions, in which every thing may be looked for," Paine wrote in the first part of *The Rights of Man*, in 1791, in England. The next year Paine wrote *Rights of Man, Part the Second*: "When, in countries that are called civilized, we see age going to the work-house and youth to the gallows, something must be wrong in the system of government." By way of remedy, Paine proposed tax tables calculated down to the last shilling, to pay for public services.[34] The first part of *Rights of Man* sold fifty thousand copies in just three months. The second part was outsold only by the Bible. But British conservatives didn't want to follow France, especially as the news from Paris grew more gruesome. Paine was charged with seditious libel. In 1792, he fled to Paris, where, as the Reign of Terror unfolded, he drafted the first part of *The Age of Reason*. In 1793, when the police knocked at his door, he handed a stash of papers to his friend, the American poet and statesman Joel Barlow. Barlow carried the manuscript to the printers; the police carried Paine to an eight-by-ten cell on the ground floor of a prison that had once been a palace. There, he would write most of the second part of *The Age of Reason* as he watched his fellow inmates go daily to their deaths. (In six weeks in the summer of 1794, Jacobins executed more than thirteen hundred people.)[35]

In *The Age of Reason*, Paine was uncompromising in his condemnation of the world's religions. Paine believed in God; he just didn't believe in scriptures; these he considered hearsay, lies, fables, and frauds that served to wreak havoc with humanity while hiding the beauty of God's creation, the evidence for which was everywhere obvious in "the universe we behold." He offered his own creed:

> I believe in one God, and no more; and I hope for happiness beyond this life. I believe in the equality of man; and I believe that religious duties consist in doing justice, loving mercy, and endeavoring to make our fellow creatures happy. But . . . I do not believe in the creed professed by the Jewish Church, by the Roman Church, by the Greek Church, by the Turkish Church, by the Protestant Church, nor by any church that I know of. My own mind is my own church.

For this, Paine was destroyed. He lost, among other things, the friendship of Samuel Adams, who had become governor of Massachusetts in 1793, when John Hancock died in office. Adams wrote to Paine, bitterly, "Do you think that your pen, or the pen of any other man, can unchristianize the mass of our citizens?"[36]

Jane Mecom died in Boston in 1794. A notice of her death in a Boston newspaper is the only time her name ever appeared in print: "Mrs. Jane Mecom, widow of the late Mr. Edward Mecom of this town and the only sister of Doctor Franklin, in the 83d year of her age."[37] What few books she owned, and most of her letters, have since been lost.

Two years later, John Adams was elected president, narrowly defeating Thomas Jefferson. Adams's administration proved controversial and inspired printers opposed to it to found seventy new papers (during Adams's term in office, newspapers grew at four times the rate of the population).[38] In Philadelphia, Benjamin Franklin Bache, Benjamin Franklin's grandson, edited the *Aurora*, a newspaper as passionately devoted to the cause of unseating John Adams from the presidency as James Franklin's *Courant* had been to tipping over Cotton Mather's pulpit.[39] In Boston, Adams's election left Benjamin Edes despairing. Edes, like Mercy Otis Warren, believed that Adams had betrayed everything the Revolution had been fought for. In 1798, Adams signed the Sedition Act, making defaming his administration a federal crime. Twenty-five people were arrested, fifteen indicted, and ten convicted, including Benjamin Franklin's grandson, who died of yellow fever before he could be brought to court.[40] Two months after passage of the Sedition Act, Edes gave up his newspaper. "I bid you FAREWELL!" he wrote, in the final issue of the *Boston Gazette*. "Maintain your Virtue—Cherish your Liberties!" He closed his shop. He moved his printing press into his house—it filled the whole of his small parlor—and tinkered with types.[41]

Jefferson defeated Adams in the election of 1800. Without the three-fifths clause, Adams would have won, which is why one Boston newspaper writer observed that Jefferson had ridden "into the temple of Liberty on the shoulders of slaves."[42] On March 4, 1801, the day after the Sedition Act expired, Thomas Jefferson was inaugurated. In his inaugural address, he talked about "the contest of opinion," a contest waged, in his lifetime, in the pages of the newspaper. Three months after Jefferson's inauguration, Edes died, destitute.

In his will, he left a single font of types to his son, Peter, who had suffered in his stead. The rest of his estate he instructed his wife to sell, to settle his debts.[43] It wasn't enough.

Thomas Paine returned to the United States in 1802, a broken man. Samuel Adams died in Boston the next year. In Paine's tortured final years, living in New Rochelle and New York City, he displayed signs of dementia. He was besieged by visitors who came either to save his soul or to damn it. He told all of them to go to hell. When an old woman announced, "I come from Almighty God to tell you that if you do not repent of your sins and believe in our blessed Savior Jesus Christ, you will be damned," Paine replied, "Pshaw. God would not send such a foolish ugly old woman as you."[44]

The longer John Adams lived, the more he hated Thomas Paine. By the end of his life, the ex-president would call *Common Sense* "a poor, ignorant, Malicious, short-sighted, Crapulous Mass." Adams also railed that the latter part of the eighteenth century had come to be called "The Age of Reason": "I am willing you should call this the Age of Frivolity, and would not object if you had named it the Age of Folly, Vice, Frenzy, Brutality, Daemons, Buonaparte, Tom Paine, or the Age of the Burning Brand from the Bottomless Pit, or anything but the Age of Reason." But even Adams admitted, "I know not whether any man in the world has had more influence on its inhabitants or affairs for the last thirty years than Tom Paine," concluding, "Call it then the Age of Paine."[45] Adams wrote those words, in 1806, as if Paine were already dead. He was not. That year, a neighbor of Paine's came across the old man himself, in a tavern in New York, so drunk and disoriented and unwashed and unkempt that his toenails had grown over his toes. Once, Paine hobbled to the polls in New Rochelle to cast his vote in a local election. He was told that he was not an American citizen and was turned away. In 1809, as the seventy-two-year-old Paine lay dying in a house in Greenwich Village, his doctor pressed him, "Do you wish to believe that Jesus Christ is the Son of God?" Paine paused, then whispered, "I have no wish to believe on that subject."[46]

"History is to ascribe the American Revolution to Thomas Paine," John Adams once complained to Thomas Jefferson.[47] It hasn't exactly worked out that way. At the end of the war, Congress asked Paine to write the history of the Revolution. He declined. Disavowed by his contemporaries, Paine left little behind in his own defense; the bulk of his papers, including notes for an autobiography, were destroyed in a fire. David Ramsay wrote about *Common Sense* admiringly, but his *History* was published before Paine's *Age of Reason*. (Ramsay, who wrote *The Life of Washington* in 1807, died in 1817 when he was shot in the back, on the streets of Charleston, by a mad tailor whom he had earlier diagnosed as dangerously insane.)[48] Mercy Otis Warren, who felt about Paine the same way Samuel Adams did, relegated the author of *Common Sense*, literally, to a footnote.[49] Warren died in Plymouth in 1814. Four years later, Paul Revere died in Boston. His obituary made no mention his ride. Neither had Ramsay or Warren, in their histories. Neither the ride nor Revere was famous until Longfellow wrote his poem in 1860—as a commentary on the coming war—after which Revere became a legend.[50] Paine's fate has been weirder. In 1800, a New York Republican Society resolved: "May his *Rights of Man* be handed down to our latest posterity, but may his *Age of Reason* never live to see the rising generation."[51] That's more or less what's happened. So wholly has *The Age of Reason* been forgotten that Paine's mantle has been claimed not only by Ronald Reagan but also by the Christian Coalition's Ralph Reed, who has quoted him, and by North Carolina senator Jesse Helms, who in 1992 supported a proposal to erect a Paine monument in Washington, DC. In 1974, Jeremy Rifkin's Peoples Bicentennial Commission published a manifesto called *Common Sense II: The Case Against Corporate Tyranny*, which, while left, not right, has a lot in common with *Glenn Beck's Common Sense: The Case Against an Out-of-Control Government.*[52] Thomas Paine, Beck once said on his show, was the Glenn Beck of the American Revolution.[53] Paine's not rolling over in his grave, though. In 1819, ten years after he was buried, his bones were dug up, and they've since been lost.[54] All things considered, that might be for the best.

The Founding Fathers, of course, had children. In 1782, John Adams's daughter became engaged to a twenty-five-year-old poet named Royall Tyler, the son of one of Boston's original Sons of Liberty, an old friend of James Otis's. Young Tyler was charming and talented. "I am not acquainted with any young Gentleman whose attainments in literature are equal to his," Abigail Adams wrote to her husband. "I am not looking out for a Poet," Adams wrote back, testily. The engagement was quietly ended.[55] Tyler next tried his hand at playwriting. *The Contrast*, the first professionally produced American play, was performed in New York while delegates to the Constitutional Convention met in Philadelphia. Overnight, Tyler became a literary celebrity. *The Contrast* is a comedy; George Washington owned two copies of it. Tyler was a wit—the "Rabelais of America," he was called. But in an age when no one could make a living as a writer (and no one wanted a poet for a son-in-law), he had to earn his keep as a lawyer. He set up a law practice in Vermont: "If writing for the public is attended with no more profit, I had rather file legal process in my attorney's office, and endeavor to explain unintelligible law to Green Mountain jurors."[56]

Tyler often wished he had chosen the ministry instead of the law, but he was sure that the dissipation of his youth would have been a blot upon the church. What he meant by his depravity is suggested by *The Origin of Evil*, a bawdy poem he published in 1793, about Adam and Eve . . .

> As her arm Eve held him hard in,
> And toy'd him with her roving hand,
> In the middle of Love's Garden,
> She saw the Tree of Knowledge stand.[57]

Tyler got past this sort of thing, or at least he didn't publish any more of it. He married in 1794, and he and his wife, Mary, raised eleven children. Mary Tyler, a celebrated midwife, was the author of an immensely popular parenting manual, *The Maternal Physician*. Four of their seven sons became clergymen. In a state where ministers were few and far between, Tyler served as a lay preacher. He often wrote and preached about religious liberty. In a sermon he delivered on Christmas Day in 1793, Tyler offered this prayer: "It is our Blessed Saviour who has caused His day spring of religious liberty from on high to visit us and that we may now worship every man according to the dictates of his own conscience."[58]

Many eighteenth-century men of letters shared Thomas Paine's views about religion, certainly his anticlericalism, and even his skepticism.[59] Very many, like Samuel Adams, most vehemently did not. And, of course, and especially outside the republic of letters, very many Americans, including Mercy Otis Warren, Phillis Wheatley, and Jane Mecom, were devout Christians. Faith, in the end, was all Jane Mecom had. Paine's views on religion were radical. But a commitment to religious liberty, religious pluralism, and the separation of church and state was not.

In 1797, Tyler published a novel called *The Algerine Captive*, about a luckless New Englander named Updike Underhill who is sold into slavery among Muslims after Barbary pirates capture the *Sympathy*. He is told that if he converts to Islam, he'll be freed. He refuses, but agrees to a debate with a mullah. "Our bible was written by men divinely inspired," Underhill says. "Our alcoran was written by the finger of the Deity himself," counters the mullah. "Our religion was disseminated in peace; yours was promulgated by the sword," Underhill insists. "The history of the christian church is a detail of bloody massacre," answers the mullah. The mullah, himself a convert, contends that Underhill, who had inherited his faith, never examined it. "Born in New England, my friend, you are a christian purified by Calvin," the mullah observes. "Born in the Campania of Rome, you had been a papist. Nursed by the Hindoos, you would have entered the pagoda with reverence, and worshipped the soul of your ancestor in a duck. Educated on the bank of the Wolga the Delai Lama had been your god. In China, you would have worshipped Tien, and perfumed Confucius, as you bowed in adoration of your ancestors."[60]

This was fiction founded in fact. In 1783, when the Treaty of Paris ended the war, American seamen lost the protection of Britain's treaties with the so-called Barbary States: Algiers, Tripoli, Morocco, and Tunisia. Over the next decade, more than seven hundred American sailors were captured and held as slaves in North Africa.[61] In Tyler's novel, Underhill holds firm. The mullah, after weeping for a man he can only see as an infidel, helps him escape. The actual end of Algerine slavery was a little different, and interestingly so. In May of 1797, just three months before *The Algerine Captive* was published, John Adams signed the Treaty of Tripoli, freeing the American captives in North Africa. Its Article 11, an assurance that the United States would never engage in a holy war, declared, in no uncertain terms, that "the Government of the United States of America is not, in any sense, founded on the Christian religion."[62]

People on the far right often argue that the idea of a "wall of separation" between church and state wasn't built until the 1830s and 1840s; Tyler was dead by then, but he seems to have thought that wall had been built at the Constitutional Convention. Invoking Islam to argue for religious liberty was an eighteenth-century commonplace, practiced by writers as different as Johnson, Montesquieu, and Voltaire, but Royall Tyler spoke and wrote about religious liberty all his life, from the pulpit, from the bench, and from his writing desk. Nor was Tyler's life a battle between reason and faith. Early and easily he reconciled his Enlightenment rationalism with his Episcopalian faith. By 1808, when Royall Tyler was chief justice of Vermont's Supreme Court, he rejected as legally invalid an out-of-state bill of sale for a slave. "Would your honor be pleased to tell us what would be sufficient evidence of my client's ownership of this man?" the lawyer asked the judge. "Oh certainly," Tyler answered wryly: a bill of sale "from the Almighty."

By 1814, Tyler had retired both from the bench and from his law professorship at the University of Vermont. Three years later, he prepared for publication a treatise called *The Touchstone; Or a Humble Modest Inquiry into the Nature of Religious Intolerance*. Here again he argued, "A State

Religion always has, and ever will be intolerant." That same year, Tyler wrote an essay in which he declared that "*all* upright ministers—all, of *every denomination*, . . . will ever condemn a connexion of church and state, as an unhallowed profanation of their character and calling."[63]

Toward the end of his life, Tyler began an autobiography. He addressed it to a reader two centuries in the future, in the year 2025: "I cannot but fancy that some profound antiquary of your superexcellent age, while groping among the rubbish of time, may from some kennel of oblivion fish up my poor book." What, he wondered, would this twenty-first-century historian make of his scrawl? Tyler pictured an historian who smiles at

> The sprawling letters, yellow text,
> The formal phrase, the bald stiff style . . .
>
> And in the margin gravely notes
> A thousand meanings never meant.

Historians, Tyler knew, will always make too much of too little. After all, what if only his left shoe made it down to that superexcellent age, "to be gathered as an invaluable treasure into the museum of the Antiquarian"? Some historians, "after vainly essaying to fit it to the right foot, would gravely declare that the anatomy of their ancestors' pedestals differed from those of his day."[64] They would think people who lived in the eighteenth century had two left feet.

EPILOGUE

Revering America

The waves that rocked them on the deep
To them their secret told.
   —Ralph Waldo Emerson, "Boston," 1873

On Sunday, April 18, 2010, three days after the Tea Party Express left Boston, George Pataki rode into town. Pataki, the former Republican governor of New York, was thinking about running for president; he was in need of a Founding Father. In Boston's North End, he positioned himself in front of an equestrian statue of Paul Revere. He was there to launch "Revere America," a nonprofit "dedicated to advancing common sense public policies rooted in our traditions of freedom and free markets that will once again make America secure and prosperous for generations to come." Its goal was "to harness and amplify the voices of the American people to give them a greater say in fighting back against the threats to freedom posed by Washington liberals." At RevereAmerica .org, you could sign a petition "to repeal and replace Obamacare" by clicking on an icon of a quill and inkwell on a piece of parchment. You could also watch a video of Pataki giving his speech to his staffers, a few passersby, and a handful of supporters. Austin Hess was in it. He was wearing his tricornered hat. He was wearing his "Don't Tread on Me" T-shirt. He was carrying a sign: "Remember in November."

"We're standing near where Paul Revere, on this day, two hundred and thirty-five years ago, began a ride," Pataki said. "He was looking to tell patriotic Americans, 'Our freedom was in danger.' We're here today to tell the people of America that once again our freedom is in danger."

I wasn't there, but I'd been there before, often; it's a place I like to go. Standing there, in front of that statue, Pataki happened to be standing where Jane Mecom's house once stood: in the 1930s, it was demolished to make room for that memorial to Paul Revere.[1]

The motto of Revere America was "Respecting Our History. Protecting Our Future." The Founding Fathers George Pataki wanted Americans to worship fought a Revolution, he believed, for the sake of free markets. That's not what the Revolution meant to Jane Mecom. In the summer of 1786, when Mecom was living in that house that would one day be demolished to make room for a statue of Paul Revere, she wrote a letter telling her brother that, in Boston, the Fourth of July—the nation's tenth birthday—was overshadowed by yet another wonderful celebration: the opening of a bridge to Cambridge. She loved the new bridge so much—"it is Really a charming Place"—that she described it for him. "As you Aproach to it it is a Beautiful Sight with a Litle Vildg at the other End the Buldings all New the Prospect on Each Side is Delight full." The day of Harvard's commencement, she told him, so many people crossed the river that the toll gatherers took in five hundred dollars. And then, musing on another crop of Harvard graduates, Jane Mecom ventured an opinion, something she didn't often do, about what it meant to have been deprived of an education, an opinion—a revolutionary opinion—about inequality. She had been reading a book by the Englishman Richard Price. "Dr Price," she reported, "thinks Thousands of Boyles Clarks and Newtons have Probably been lost to the world, and lived and died in Ignorance and meanness, merely for want of being Placed in favourable Situations, and Injoying Proper Advantages." Thousands of Isaac Newtons were out there, living and dying in poverty, ignorance, and obscurity. The chances for escape weren't good. "Very few we know," she reminded her brother, "is able to beat thro all Impediments and Arive to any Grat Degre of superiority in Understanding."[2]

Her brother didn't need reminding. Every letter his sister wrote to him contained this truth. Benjamin Franklin carried his family in his blood and his sister on his back. He must have thought about this a great deal. He began his autobiography by explaining why he was taking the trouble to write the story of his life: "Having emerg'd from the Poverty & Obscurity in which I was born & bred, to a State of Affluence & some Degree of Reputation in the World, and having gone so far thro' Life with a considerable Share of Felicity, the conducing Means I made use of, which, the Blessing of God, so well succeeded, my Posterity may like to know, as they may find some of them suitable to their own Situations, & therefore fit to be imitated."[3] He wrote, in other words, to answer the question with which everyone he met must have pestered him: How, for God's sake, how on earth, Dr. Franklin, pray, tell me, did you, the tenth son of a second-rate chandler, manage to escape from poverty and obscurity?

In the world into which Franklin and his sister were born, very few beat through. Of their father's seventeen children, Benjamin was the only one. That world was changing. Massachusetts had already abolished slavery. In 1789, Boston, for the first time, mandated the education of girls.[4] Franklin's escape, America's birth, an age of revolutions, made possible a new world, a world of fewer obstacles. Franklin liked to think of his life as the story of America, and in a way, he was right. He never finished his autobiography. And maybe that's because he knew that, since he had made his life into an allegory for America, it could have no ending. The Revolution is the story of America because it is a story of beginning.

The day after George Pataki came to Boston was Patriot's Day, which has been a Massachusetts state holiday since 1969. The nineteenth of April was also the day of the Boston Marathon, and, for a long time, it was the day of the Red Sox home opener. There was also an annual reenactment of the Battle of Lexington and Concord, but it started at dawn, and, in my house, we had never once managed to get out of bed fast enough to make it there in time. We shambled, and breakfasted, and then biked from Cambridge to Lexington along the Minuteman Bicycle Path. By the time we got there, the battle was over, but costumed reenactors were still wandering around, waiting for the parade to start. Late but undefeated, we bought, from a street vendor on Massachusetts Avenue, a small arsenal of cheap wooden muskets and, recruiting some other sleepy-headed colonials, waged our own battle on the green. The redcoats, leaning against a stand of trees, gave every appearance of being undaunted by our assault. Bloody lobsterbacks. Then we ate hamburgers and talked about the men who had died on that spot, all those years ago, and what they died for. By then, we had all gotten a little weary of Longfellow—"Listen, my children, and you shall hear"—but once you commit a thing to memory, it gets stuck there:

For, borne on the night-wind of the Past,
Through all our history, to the last,

In the hour of darkness and peril and need,
The people will waken and listen to hear
The hurrying hoof-beats of that steed,
And the midnight message of Paul Revere.[5]

We had another musket fight. It got pretty fierce. We ate some ice cream. We biked home, thinking about the night-wind of the past.

What was the Revolution about? What is history for? Who are we? I tried to stop watching, but every story in the news seemed to ask the same questions. On April 23, Arizona governor Jan Brewer signed into law a bill making the failure to carry immigration documents a crime and authorizing police to question anyone who might possibly be an illegal immigrant.[6] Five days later, Jeff Perry, a Republican from Cape Cod, introduced an amendment in the Massachusetts legislature to deny public assistance to illegal immigrants. With Palin gone, the Boston Tea Party turned its attention to planning a "Pass the Perry Amendment" rally.[7] (Perry had also introduced, in 2009, the Massachusetts Tenth Amendment Resolution. Tenth Amendment resolutions, asserting state sovereignty and opposing the expansion of the federal government, had been introduced in forty states and had passed in four.)[8]

On April 30, Glenn Beck launched a series called "Founders' Fridays." He began with Samuel Adams. He lamented the founders' fall from greatness: "Our Founding Fathers were once revered in this country as divinely inspired, courageous visionaries. But now, after the past one hundred years of 'enlightenment,' we've come to realize that they were nothing but old, white, racist, heathens." He explained his purpose: "In order to restore the country, we have to restore the men who founded it on certain principles to the rightful place in our national psyche."[9] On the next Founders' Friday, May 7, Beck reported that the ratings were so good during that first show that he was thinking about extending the series. "It seems like America, for some reason or another, is interested now in our Founding Fathers and meeting who they really, truly are." He introduced his guests, Earl Taylor, president of the National Center for Constitutional Studies, and Andrew Allison, coauthor of *The Real George Washington*. He urged viewers to read Washington's own words. "When you read these guys," Beck said, "it's alive. It's like, you know, reading the scriptures. It's like reading the Bible. It is alive today. And it only comes alive when you need it."[10] Just like Jesus in the Gospels.

That same day, and also on Fox News, Bill O'Reilly interviewed Sarah Palin. "Why do you think America is a Christian nation?" O'Reilly asked. "Nobody has to believe me," Palin said. "You can just go to our Founding Fathers' early documents and see how they crafted a Declaration of Independence and a Constitution that allows that Judeo-Christian belief to be the foundation of our lives." O'Reilly, playing devil's advocate, suggested that some people might say that the United States had changed, "and now we're a much more secular nation than we were back in 1776." Palin called that kind of thinking "an attempt to revisit and rewrite history." She wanted to "go back to what our founders and our founding documents meant. They're quite clear that we would create law based on the God of the Bible and the Ten Commandments."[11] Take back Washington. Take back America. Take back the past.

I thought about Langston Hughes:

O, let America be America again—
The land that never has been yet.[12]

On May 11, the executive board of the nine-thousand-member Organization of American Historians passed a resolution urging the Texas School Board to reconsider its proposed amendments to the state's social studies curriculum and instead "adopt a history curriculum that reflects the understanding of history developed by the historians and history teachers of Texas."[13] Similar statements were issued by, among other organizations, the National Council for History Education.[14] These resolutions, though, were hardly likely to exert an influence, given the views board members held about the historical profession. The day the Organization of American Historians released that statement, the governor of Arizona signed into law a bill prohibiting the state's public schools from offering courses in ethnic studies. The new bill was targeted at a Mexican American studies program in the Tucson school district that, according to the Associated Press, was believed by the state's head of public education to teach "Latino students that they are oppressed by white people."[15]

When the Texas School Board convened on May 18, its meeting opened with remarks by Cynthia Dunbar, a Republican member of the board with a degree from Pat Robertson's Regent University School of Law and who was, at the time, a visiting professor of law at Liberty University, an evangelical school in Virginia. Dunbar prayed,

> I believe that no one can read the history of our country without realizing that the Good Book and the Spirit of the Savior have, from the beginning, been our guiding geniuses. Whether we look to the first Charter of Virginia, or the Charter of New England, or the Charter of Massachusetts Bay, or the Fundamental Orders of Connecticut, the same objective is present—a Christian land, governed by Christian principles. I believe the entire Bill of Rights came into being because of the knowledge our forefathers had of the

Bible, and their belief in it: freedom of belief, of expression, of assembly, of petition; the dignity of the individual; the sanctity of the home; equal justice under law; and the reservations of powers to the people. I like to believe we are living today in the spirit of the Christian religion. I like also to believe that as long as we do so, no great harm can come to our country. All this I pray, in the name of my Lord and Savior, Jesus Christ. Amen.[16]

Why bother fighting over school prayer when you can teach evangelical Christianity in history class? For Dunbar, who leapt from the New Testament to the New World and then collapsed the nearly two centuries separating Virginia's royal charter and the Bill of Rights, as if James I were the same man as James Madison, history *was* religion.

All week, while public hearings were held in Austin about the set of history standards known as Texas Essential Knowledge and Skills (or TEKS), the Tea Party was in the news. On Tuesday, Rand Paul, Ron Paul's son, won a Kentucky primary for a U.S. Senate seat, running as a member of the Tea Party. When the Texas School Board met in Austin on Wednesday, the Texas NAACP held a protest rally outside, called "Don't White-Out Our History." Inside, Benjamin Jealous, national president of the NAACP, said, "We wake up every morning, and try to push our country forward, not trying to keep it from running backwards. And this, my mom, reading through these TEKS with me, a very well-educated woman, says, 'This is taking us in a direction toward the way I was taught in the 1940s.'"[17] That night, on MSNBC, Rand Paul talked about his reservations about the 1964 Civil Rights Act. Rachel Maddow asked him, "Do you think that a private business has the right to say we don't serve black people?" Paul hemmed and hawed.[18]

The Texas School Board was scheduled to vote on Friday. That morning, I went to a public school in my neighborhood to visit a third-grade classroom, where the kids, including one of mine, were studying the Revolution.

Jocelyn Marshall handed out folders to each of six groups of kids.

"Lexington and Concord, can you come up and get your stuff? I got you guys maps."

After they grabbed their folders, the kids gathered around their desks, sitting in chairs whose feet were covered with tennis balls, to hush the sound of scraping.

"Boston Massacre, right here." Three boys came up.

"Can I also have, Battle of Bunker Hill? Battle of Bunker Hill!"

"And remember, Boston Tea Party," Marshall shouted out the door, "I'm letting you work in the hallway, but please don't make me regret it."

The kids were using a textbook called *Massachusetts: Our Home*. Marshall had also brought in a whole library of books. They'd been researching, mining sources, and now they were writing scripts for a video they were going to be making, a television newscast. Each group was supposed to have at least one news anchor, field reporter, and eyewitness.

Julie, Charlotte, and Fiona were Taxation without Representation, and they were way ahead of everyone else. They'd finished their script, days before, and were already rehearsing.

JULIE: Hello I'm Julie and this is *Colonial Times Today*. We are here to tell you about Massachusetts in the 1760s. Here is Charlotte to tell you more about taxation without representation.

CHARLOTTE: Thank you, Julie. Here in Massachusetts we're experiencing strong emotion about the taxes issued from

England. People are being taxed on sugar, molasses, stamps, glass, and even tea. (*Turning to Fiona.*) This is Fiona, with her strong opinion. Now tell us Fiona, do you think the king is taxing you unfairly?

FIONA: Of course I do! He's taxing us on silly things like stamps. That's *ridiculous*!!!!!

This, I guess, was the belly of the beast, the alarming left-wing lunacy, the godless irreverence, the socialist political indoctrination taught in the public schools of the People's Republic of Cambridge: an assignment that requires research, that raises questions about perspective, that demands distinctions between fact and opinion, that bears an audience in mind—an assignment that teaches the art of historical writing.

"Hey, Fiona!" Simon had wandered over. "What else did they tax besides tea and paper?"

"Oh, I've got a whole list." She reached into her folder. "Look!"

Earlier in the year, the class had studied the Pilgrims, building colonial houses and Wampanoag wigwams out of hay and mud, and I had learned that if you put a marshmallow on top of a Girl Scout mint cookie, cover the whole thing with chocolate sauce, let it harden, and stick a butterscotch Lifesaver on it, for the buckle, it makes a pretty good Pilgrim hat. Fiona had been a star of the Pilgrim unit. In a skit on animal husbandry, she stole the show, playing, by turns, a pig, a sheep, and a chicken. She turned to Charlotte and Julie, "I think I should do this when I say, 'ridiculous.'" She crossed her arms in front of her chest and pouted.

Julie shook her head. "That king must have been insane."

I followed Simon back to the Boston Massacre, where there was much talk of Crispus Attucks.

Peter, leaning over his desk, suggested, "How about we have him say, 'When I ran away from Framingham, I became a ropemaker'?"

Most of what happens is forgotten. Most of the past is lost, gone the way of Benjamin Edes's spectacles and Phillis Wheatley's unpublished poems and James Otis's papers and Thomas Paine's bones and Royall Tyler's right shoe and Jane Mecom's house. Historians sometimes rescue things. I pictured William Cooper Nell, digging in the archives and discovering that runaway ad from the *Boston Gazette*, and I was glad it had made its way, down through the years, and onto Peter's desk.

"Right," agreed Simon. "Because, remember, he's mad at the British soldiers because they started taking his job."

The study of history requires investigation, imagination, empathy, and respect. Reverence just doesn't enter into it.

Jazire, who has silver-rimmed, Franklinian glasses and who used to have a mohawk, but which was growing back in, was going to get to play Attucks, who was going to be their eyewitness. He was taking everything down with a black Sharpie. I asked him how he was going to be interviewed, given that he was killed during the massacre.

"No, that's the good part," he said, grinning. "In the middle of the interview, I get shot!"

In the hallway, the Boston Tea Partiers were lying on their stomachs on linoleum tiles of speckled blue, writing out cue cards on giant sheets of white-lined paper. Lucy and Zeyla were planning to be coanchors. They practiced their head-of-the-hour patter.

ZEYLA: How's that tea doing today?
LUCY: Speaking of tea . . .
ZEYLA (*to the camera*): It's November 3, 1773, Boston, Massachusetts.

LUCY: Samuel Adams said the Sons of Liberty should do something other than just talk. (*cut to field reporter*)

MAGGIE: Here I am on the wharf.

I asked Jeffte, who was waiting his turn to be the eyewitness, what he thought the Boston Tea Party was about.

"It was about taxes," he said, while running laps up and down the hall. I didn't think the Tea Party had much chance of getting to work in the hallway again. "They were taxing them on everything. If they were sitting in a chair"—he pointed to a chair, leaning against a wall, as he ran past it—"they would tax the chair."

I headed back into the classroom. Nathalie and Sophia were glum about their project, which, it must be said, lacked a certain dramatic potential. They had to talk about four famous patriots. Their script was coming along, though, and they had found out some good stuff. "First up is John Adams, the second president. He wanted George Washington to lead the American troops. Did you know he was the lawyer for the British after the Boston Massacre? He believed everybody should get a fair trial."

Lexington and Concord was revising a first draft. "Good morning! It's April 20, 1775, on *Colonial Times Today*. Breaking news: the American Revolution has begun!"

I went over to the Battle of Bunker Hill. Grace was stage crafting.

"We're going to have the field reporter be in, like, on a fake hill, and then—"

"A fake hill?" asked Josh. "How are we going to make that?"

There was a teacher's assistant at the table.

"I have a feeling this group needs to do a little bit more research."

The kids in this school, who come in every color, come from a lot of different places. Haider was from Pakistan and had only just got here. He was sitting on a rug, leaning against a bookshelf, writing. He was working on the Declaration of Independence. I asked him what the Revolution was about. He took a minute to think.

"At first, the United States wasn't a country. They were with the British. And so the Declaration of Independence was made because Thomas Jefferson wanted the colonies to be free and he wanted the British to be a country, so they could live in their own country."

I walked home to watch the news out of Austin, thinking how much I'd rather watch *Colonial Times Today* and wondering what would make a good Revolutionary snack. Later that day, the Texas School Board voted to approve nearly all the proposed amendments to its social studies curriculum. That curriculum will be revised again, one day soon. More things, too, are certain. In American politics, the story of the nation's founding will be resurrected again and again, put to one use, and then another. A generation of historians will grow up and grow old. And I will hold dear, forever, the memory of a nine-year-old boy, sitting on a rug, quietly writing history.

The Revolution was a beginning; the battle over its meaning can have no ending. When I got on board the *Beaver* in Gloucester one raw winter's morning, I remembered I had been on that ship before; in an attic somewhere, there must be a picture of me on a third-grade field trip, a red, white, and blue bicentennial feather in my Red Sox hat, standing on a crate marked TEA. There was no tea there anymore. In the bottom of the hull, bilgewater sloshed past a pile of rusty pulleys. Scattered from bow to stern were the remnants of work, interrupted: C-clamps, eyebolts, sheaves of plywood, a rumpled canvas, and a can of WD-40, missing its cap. A coil of rope occupied a bench. Down below, the ship's rudder was bound with rope, held fast against the ocean's everyday sway and the magnificent violence of each passing storm.

ACKNOWLEDGMENTS

Eighteenth-century books didn't have acknowledgments, or not exactly, so maybe this book shouldn't either. Except, thank goodness, the eighteenth century is over. Thanks, first, to Henry Finder at *The New Yorker*. Thanks to Brigitta van Rheinberg at Princeton University Press and to Ruth O'Brien at the Public Square. Thanks to Tina Bennett, as ever. Thanks to six historians who read the manuscript: Richard D. Brown, Eric Foner, Michael Klarman, James Kloppenberg, Jack Rakove, and Alfred F. Young. And thanks to six who commented on an earlier essay: Vincent Brown, John Demos, Tony Horwitz, Jane Kamensky, Bruce Schulman, and Laurel Thatcher Ulrich. Thanks to members of the Boston Tea Party, who, knowing that we disagreed about very many things, took the time to talk with me, and thanks, too, to everyone I spoke with at the Old State House, the Old South Meeting House, Historic Tours of America, and the Gloucester Marine Railways. Heartfelt thanks to Jocelyn Marshall and her crackerjack third-grade class. Thanks to Hannah Goldfield and Christopher Glazek, for checking facts, and to J. C. Bell, Benjamin Carp, and Ray Raphael, for answers. For lickety-split last-minute assistance in the archives in the final days of writing this book, thanks to Latif Nasser, Natalie Panno, Bernard Zipprich, and especially Emily Graff. To everyone in my house, I promise: no more tea. Thanks, finally, to my students, who make the Revolution interesting all over again, every time it rolls around.

Jill Lepore
Cambridge, Massachusetts
June 17, 2010
The 235th anniversary of
the Battle of Bunker Hill

NOTES

Prologue: Party Like It's 1773

[1] John J. Currier, *History of Newburyport, Mass.*, *1764–1905* (New-buryport, MA, 1906), 66; Eleanor C. Parson, *Thachers: Island of the Twin Lights* (Canaan, NH: Phoenix, 1985), 13–17. My thanks to Leon Poindexter and Viking Gustafson for permission to board the *Beaver*.

[2] Fred Pillsbury, "1973 Tea Ship Beaver II Had Rough Time Making It Here," *Boston Globe*, December 16, 1973; Rick Klein, "After Blaze, Gift Shop Is History: Tea Party Museum, Ship Closed for Now," *Boston Globe*, August 5, 2001; Javier C. Hernandez and Andrew Ryan, "Boston Tea Party Museum Catches Fire," *Boston Globe*, August 27, 2007; Javier C. Hernandez, "Boston Tea Party Museum Catches Fire Again," *Boston Globe*, August 28, 2007.

[3] Rick Santelli, *Squawk Box*, CNBC, New York, February 19, 2009.

[4] Ralph Waldo Emerson, "The Concord Hymn," in *The Complete Works of Ralph Waldo Emerson*, ed. Edward Waldo Emerson (Boston: Houghton Mifflin, 1904), 9:158. On Emerson's grandfather, see Robert A. Gross, *The Minutemen and Their World* (New York: Hill and Wang, 1976), 1:120.

[5] See, e.g., "Protestors Gather for Self-Styled Tea Party," Fox News, Chicago, February 27, 2009.

[6] Liz Robbins, "Tax Day Is Met with Tea Parties," *New York Times*, April 15, 2009; Boston Tea Party 2009, weblog, April 22, 2009, http://teapartyboston2009.blogspot.com/.

[7] William Safire, *Safire's Political Dictionary*, rev. ed. (New York: Oxford University Press, 2008), 659–60.

[8] Annette Gordon-Reed, *The Hemingses of Monticello: An American Family* (New York: Norton, 2008).

[9] Joe Biesk, "Thousands in U.S. Protest Tax Day with 'Tea Parties,'" Associated Press, April 16, 2009.

[10] Sean Hannity, *The Hannity Show*, Fox News, New York, April 15, 2009.

[11]Thomas Paine, *The Age of Reason* (Boston: Thomas Hall, 1794), 6.

[12]Robbins, "Tax Day Is Met with Tea Parties"; "Tea Parties Protest Government Spending," slide show, *New York Times*, April 15, 2009; Michael E. Ruane, "D.C. Tax Protest Is No Tea Party," *Washington Post*, April 16, 2009; Biesk, "Thousands in U.S. Protest Tax Day."

[13]Henry Wadsworth Longfellow, "Paul Revere's Ride," in *The Children's Hour and Other Poems: Paul Revere's Ride and Other Poems* (Boston: Houghton, Mifflin, 1894), 1–6. On Revere's place in history and memory, see David Hackett Fischer, *Paul Revere's Ride* (New York: Oxford University Press, 1994); and Ray Raphael, *Founding Myths: Stories That Hide Our Patriotic Past* (New York: New Press, 2004), chap. 1.

[14]Michael McDonald, "Voter Turnout," United States Elections Project, http://elections.gmu.edu/index.html; Carl Hulse, "No Surprises in Electoral Tally," *New York Times*, January 9, 2009; John Harwood, "Obama, with a Pile of Chips," *New York Times*, February 14, 2009.

[15]George Ticknor Curtis, *The True Uses of American Revolutionary History* (Boston, 1841), 1, 7–8.

[16]Hannity, *The Hannity Show*, Fox News, May 6, 2009. On the history of the liberty tree, see Alfred F. Young, "Liberty Tree: Made in America, Lost in America," in *Liberty Tree: Ordinary People and the American Revolution* (New York: New York University Press, 2006), 325–94.

[17]John Ridpath, "John Ridpath at the July 4 Boston Tea Party Protest," video recording, ARCTV.com, July 14, 2009, http://arc-tv.com/john-ridpath-at-the-july-4-boston-tea-party-protest/.

[18]Hannity, *The Hannity Show*, Fox News, New York, September 2, 2009; Glenn Beck, *The Glenn Beck Show*, Fox News, New York, September 2, 2009; Judy Keen and Greg Toppo, "Planned Obama Speech to Students Sparks Protest," *USA Today*, September 1, 2009; Barack Obama, "Prepared Remarks of President Barack Obama: Back to School Event," September 8, 2008, http://www.whitehouse.gov/media resources/preparedschoolremarks/; Sam Dillon, "Presidential Pep Talk Ticks Off Year for Students," *New York Times*, September 8, 2009. For CNN coverage, see http://edition.cnn.com/2009/POLITICS/09/08/obama.school.speech/index.html.

[19]Joseph Andrew Stack, from "Joe Stack Statement: Alleged Suicide Note from Austin Pilot Posted Online," *Huffington Post*, February 18, 2010, http://www.huffingtonpost.com/2010/02/18/joe-stack-statement-alleg_n_467539.html.

[20]Glenn Beck, *The Glenn Beck Show*, Fox News, New York, March 5, 2010.

[21]The reenactment at the Old State House is run by the Bostonian Society and the National Park Service; I have worked as a consultant for both.

[22]Hannah McBride, "Boston Massacre Event Gives Youths New View of History," *Boston Globe*, March 7, 2010.

[23]James C. McKinley Jr., "Texas Conservatives Seek Deeper Stamp on Texts," *New York Times*, March 10, 2010.

[24]James C. McKinley Jr., "Texas Conservatives Win Curriculum Change," *New York Times*, March 12, 2010; Texas State Board of Education (TSBE), "Proposed Revisions to 19 TAC Chapter 113, Texas Essential Knowledge and Skills for Social Studies, Subchapter A, Elementary," Texas Education Agency (TEA), April 2010, http://ritter.tea.state .tx.us/teks/social/ELEM_TEKS_1stRdg.pdf; TSBE, "Proposed Revisions to 19 TAC Chapter 113, Texas Essential Knowledge and Skills for Social Studies, Subchapter B, Middle School," TEA, April 2010, http://ritter.tea.state.tx.us/teks/social/MS_TEKS_1stRdg.pdf; TSBE, "Proposed Revisions to 19 TAC Chapter 113, Texas Essential Knowledge and Skills for Social Studies (hereafter TEKS), Subchapter C, High School," TEA, April 2010, http://ritter.tea.state.tx.us/teks/social/HS_ TEKS_1stRdg.pdf.

[25]TSBE, "113.13. Social Studies Kindergarten, Section B, Point 2," in "Subchapter A, Elementary," 2; TSBE, "113.13. Social Studies, Grade 2, Section B, Point 9b," in "Subchapter A, Elementary," 13; TSBE, "113.20 Social Studies, Grade 8, Section B, Point 12b," in "Subchapter B, Middle School," 25; TSBE, "113.41 Social Studies, United States History Studies Since 1877, Section C, Point 8.B, Point 9.E," 5–7; TSBE, "113.41, 113.42 World History Studies, Section C, Point 20.C," 23; TSBE, "113.41 Social Studies, United States History Studies Since 1877, Point 24," in "Subchapter C, High School," 10; TSBE, "113.44 United States Government, Section C, Point 1.B," in "Subchapter C, High School," 38; TSBE, "113.44 United States Government, Section C, Point 1.C," in "Subchapter C, High School," 39.

[26]Milton Terris, "An Early System of Compulsory Health Insurance," *Bulletin of the History of Medicine* 10 (May 1944): 433–44; and see the discussion in Odin W. Anderson, *The Uneasy Equilibrium: Private and Public Financing of Health Services in the United States, 1875–1965* (New Haven, CT: College and University Press, 1968), 21–22.

[27]On anti-intellectualism, including its relationship to populism, see Richard Hofstadter, *Anti-Intellectualism in American Life* (New

York: Knopf, 1963). On history as conspiracy, see Richard Hofstadter, *The Age of Reform: From Bryan to F.D.R.* (New York: Vintage Books, 1955), 70–81.

[28]Many scholars have written about what Robert Bellah called a "civil religion" ("Civil Religion," *Daedalus* 96 [1967]: 1–21), while others have examined the ways in which Americans have often taken the founding documents as matters of faith, including Pauline Maier, *American Scripture: Making the Declaration of Independence* (New York: Knopf, 1997); and Michael Kammen, *A Machine That Would Go of Itself: The Constitution in American Culture* (New York: Knopf, 1986).

[29]Warren G. Harding, "Inaugural Address: Friday, March 4, 1921," in *Fellow Citizens: The Penguin Book of U.S. Presidential Addresses*, ed. Robert Vincent Remini (New York: Penguin Group, 2008), 298; Richard B. Bernstein, *The Founding Fathers Reconsidered* (New York: Oxford University Press, 2009), 3–4. Harding had earlier referred to "founding American fathers" (1912) and "American founding fathers" (1916). H. L. Mencken, "Gamalielese," in *On Politics: A Carnival of Buncombe*, ed. Malcolm Moos (Baltimore: John Hopkins University Press, 1956), 42.

[30]*The Spirit of Seventy-Six; Or, the Coming Woman* (Boston: Little, Brown, 1868), 51. What leads the founders to wake from the dead is always changing. In 1920, it was Woodrow Wilson ("fast leading the country to the eternal bowwows"): "Washington and the fathers are turning in their graves" ("Keynote and Platform," *Cleveland Plain Dealer*, June 9, 1920).

[31]Turning: *Cobbett's Weekly Register*, August 20, 1825, 470; rolling over: Robert Harborough Sherard, *A Bartered Honour* (London, 1883), 138. With thanks to Caitlin Galante-DeAngelis Hopkins.

[32]Washington Irving, "The Legend of Sleepy Hollow" in *The Sketchbook of Geoffrey Crayon, Gent.* (New York: G. P. Putnam, 1864), 455.

[33]For a reflection on this subject, see Charles Beard, "Written History as an Act of Faith," *American Historical Review* 39 (1933): 219–31.

Chapter 1: Ye Olde Media

[1]The Scallywag was sold by a hat company called elope, based in Colorado Springs.

[2]Austin Hess, e-mail message to the author, March 23, 2010.

³John Adams to Thomas Jefferson and Thomas McKean, July 30, 1815, and Thomas Jefferson to John Adams, August 10, 1815, *The Adams-Jefferson Letters: The Complete Correspondence between Thomas Jefferson and John and Abigail Adams*, ed. Lester J. Cappon (Chapel Hill: University of North Carolina Press, 1959), 2:451–52.

⁴Oliver's history wasn't published until 1961. Peter Oliver, *Origin and Progress of the American Rebellion: A Tory View*, ed. Douglas Adair and John A. Schulz (San Marino: Huntington Library, 1961). See also Linda Ayers, "Peter Oliver's Portrait Gallery," in *Harvard Divided* (Cambridge, MA: Harvard University Press, 1976), 17–40.

⁵David Ramsay, *The History of the American Revolution* (Philadelphia, 1789), 2:323.

⁶Thomas Jefferson to Williams Stephens Smith, November 13, 1787, *The Papers of Thomas Jefferson*, ed. Julian Boyd (Princeton, NJ: Princeton University Press, 1950), 12:356.

⁷Garry Wills, *A Necessary Evil: A History of American Distrust of Government* (New York: Simon and Schuster, 1999), 205.

⁸William Pencak, "Samuel Adams and Shays' Rebellion," *New England Quarterly* 62 (1989): 64; Marvin Meyers, "Founding and Revolution: A Commentary on Publius-Madison," in *The Hofstadter Aegis: A Memorial*, ed. Stanley Elkins and Eric McKitrick (New York: Knopf, 1974), 35.

⁹A suggestive collection is Philip Foner, ed., *We, the Other People: Alternative Declarations of Independence by Labor Groups, Farmers, Woman's Rights Advocates, Socialists, and Blacks, 1829–1975* (Urbana: University of Illinois Press, 1976).

¹⁰"Divergent Views of Public Men," *Life*, September 17, 1956, 119–20. Martin Luther King Jr., "Love, Law, and Civil Disobedience (1961)," in *A Testament of Hope: The Essential Writings of Martin Luther King*, ed. James Melvin Washington (San Francisco: HarperSanFrancisco, 1991), 50. Lyndon B. Johnson, Special Message to the Congress, March 15, 1965, *Public Papers of the Presidents of the United States: Lyndon B. Johnson, 1965* (Washington, DC: Government Printing Office, 1966), 1:281. *Washington Afro-American*, September 20, 1966.

¹¹John E. Bodnar, *Remaking America: Public Memory, Patriotism, and Commemoration in Twentieth-Century America* (Princeton, NJ: Princeton University Press, 1992), 229. On the Bicentennial, see American Revolution Bicentennial Administration (ARBA), *The Bicentennial of the United States of America: A Final Report to the People*, 5 vols. (Washington, DC: Government Printing Office, 1977).

Massachusetts had formed its own bicentennial commission in 1964 (ARBA, *Bicentennial of the United States of America*, 1:58). On memory and the Revolution, see also David Lowenthal, "The Bicentennial Landscape: A Mirror Held Up to the Past," *Geographical Review* 67 (1977): 253–67; Milton M. Klein, "Commemorating the American Revolution: The Bicentennial and Its Predecessors," *New York History* 58 (1977): 257–76; Michael G. Kammen, *A Season of Youth: The American Revolution and the Historical Imagination* (New York: Knopf, 1978); and Alfred F. Young, *The Shoemaker and the Tea Party: Memory and the American Revolution* (Boston: Beacon Press, 1981). On history and memory, more broadly, see David Lowenthal, *The Past Is a Foreign Country* (Cambridge: Cambridge University Press, 1985).

[12]Martin Luther King Jr., "Where Do We Go from Here? (1967)," in *A Call to Conscience: The Landmark Speeches of Dr. Martin Luther King, Jr.*, ed. Clayborne Carson and Chris Shepherd (New York: IPM, 2001), 182.

[13]John Adams to Thomas Jefferson, August 24, 1815, in *Adams-Jefferson Letters*, 2:455.

[14]Oliver, *Origin and Progress*, 9.

[15]Accounts of Boston in the 1760s and 1770s include Carl Bridenbaugh, *Cities in Revolt: Urban Life in America, 1743–1776* (New York: Knopf, 1955); Gary Nash, *Urban Crucible: The Northern Seaports and the Origins of the American Revolution* (Cambridge, MA: Harvard University Press, 1986); and Benjamin Carp, *Rebels Rising: Cities and the American Revolution* (Oxford: Oxford University Press, 2007). On the fire, see William Pencak, "The Social Structure of Revolutionary Boston: Evidence from the Great Fire of 1760," *Journal of Interdisciplinary History* 10 (Autumn 1979): 267–78. On the effects of the French and Indian War, see Fred Anderson, *A People's Army: Massachusetts Soldiers and Society and the Seven Years' War* (Chapel Hill: University of North Carolina Press, 1984).

[16]On Otis, see William Tudor, *The Life of James Otis of Massachusetts* (Boston, 1823). On Bernard: Colin Nicholson, *The "Infamas Govener": Francis Bernard and the Origins of the American Revolution* (Boston: Northeastern University Press, 2000). But the best account of the conflicts among these men can be found in Bernard Bailyn's masterful study, *The Ordeal of Thomas Hutchinson* (Cambridge, MA: Harvard University Press, 1974).

[17]"Portraiture in the Old State House" and "Furnishings in the Old State House," typescript, Old State House Files, Bostonian Society, Boston.

[18]John Adams to William Tudor, March 29, 1817, *The Works of John Adams*, ed. Charles Francis Adams (1856; repr., New York: Arno Press, 1971), 10:247. See also James M. Farrell, "The Writs of Assistance and Public Memory: John Adams and the Legacy of James Otis," *New England Quarterly* 79 (2006): 533–66.

[19]On Wheatley's life, see William H. Robinson, *Phillis Wheatley and Her Writings* (New York: Garland, 1984); and Phillis Wheatley, *Complete Writings*, ed. Vincent Carretta (New York: Penguin, 2001). A traveler's account of the harbor is reprinted in Horace E. Scudder, "Life in Boston in the Provincial Period," in *The Memorial History of Boston*, ed. Justin Winsor (Boston, 1882), 2:440.

[20]Robinson, *Wheatley*, 8.

[21]*Boston Gazette*, July 13, 1761; Henry Louis Gates, *The Trials of Phillis Wheatley: America's First Black Poet and Her Encounters with the Founding Fathers* (New York: Basic Civitas Books, 2000), 17.

[22]Wheatley, "To His Excellency General Washington," in *Complete Writings*, 89.

[23]Mercy Otis Warren, *History of the Rise, Progress and Termination of the American Revolution*, ed. Lester Cohen (1805; repr., Indianapolis: Liberty Classics, 1988), 1:xliii. On Warren, see Nancy Rubin Stuart, *The Muse of the Revolution: The Secret Pen of Mercy Otis Warren and the Founding of the Revolution* (Boston: Beacon, 2008); and Rosemarie Zagarri, *A Woman's Dilemma: Mercy Otis Warren and the American Revolution* (Wheeling, IL: Harlan Davidson, 1995). A valuable sample of Warren's correspondence is Mercy Otis Warren, *Mercy Otis Warren: Selected Letters*, ed. Jeffrey H. Richards and Sharon M. Harris (Athens: University of Georgia Press, 2009).

[24]John Dickinson, "An Address to 'Friends and Countrymen' on the Stamp Act (1765)," in *Memoirs of the Historical Society of Pennsylvania* 14 (1895): 204.

[25]On this relationship, see David Waldstreicher, *Slavery's Constitution: From Revolution to Ratification* (New York: Norton, 2008).

[26]Stephen Hopkins, *The Rights of the Colonies Examined* (Providence, RI: William Goddard, 1764), 4.

[27]James Otis, *The Rights of the British Colonies* (Boston: Edes and Gill, 1764), 4, 29.

[28]*Boston Gazette* October 14, 1765. On the Stamp Act, see Edmund S. Morgan and Helen M. Morgan, *The Stamp Act Crisis: Prologue to Revolution* (New York: Collier Books, 1963). On the resistance movement, see Pauline Maier, *From Resistance to Revolution:*

Colonial Radicals and the Development of American Opposition to Britain, 1765–1776 (New York: Knopf, 1972).

²⁹On the early history of newsletters, newsbooks, and newspapers, see Joad Raymond, *The Invention of the Newspaper: English Newsbooks, 1641–1649* (Oxford: Oxford University Press, 2005); Charles E. Clark, *The Public Prints: The Newspaper in Anglo-American Culture, 1665–1740* (New York: Oxford University Press, 1994); and James Raven, *The Business of Books: Booksellers and the English Book Trade, 1450–1850* (New Haven, CT: Yale University Press, 2007), especially chap. 9. On the early history of American newspapers, see John Hench, ed., *Three Hundred Years of American Newspapers* (Worcester, MA: American Antiquarian Society, 1990); Isaiah Thomas, *The History of Printing in America*, 2 vols. (Albany,1874); Clarence S. Brigham, *A History and Bibliography of American Newspapers* (Worcester, 1947); David A. Copeland, *Colonial American Newspapers: Character and Content* (Newark: University of Delaware Press, 1997); John Tebbel, *The Compact History of the American Newspaper*, rev. ed. (New York: Hawthorn Books, 1969); Richard D. Brown, *Knowledge Is Power: The Diffusion of Information in Early America, 1700–1865* (New York: Oxford University Press, 1989); David Paul Nord, *Communities of Journalism: A History of American Newspapers and Their Readers* (Urbana: University of Illinois Press, 2001); and Eric Burns, *Infamous Scribblers: The Founding Fathers and the Rowdy Beginnings of American Journalism* (New York: Public Affairs, 2006).

³⁰On the making of newspapers, see Lawrence Wroth, *The Colonial Printer* (New York: Grolier Club, 1931); and Jeffrey L. Pasley, *The Tyranny of Printers: Newspaper Politics in the Early American Republic* (Charlottesville: University Press of Virginia, 2001).

³¹On the importance of the *New-England Courant*, see Perry Miller, introduction to *The New-England Courant: A Selection of Certain Issues* (Boston: Academy of Arts and Sciences, 1956), 5–9; Nord, *Communities of Journalism*, 52; and Thomas C. Leonard, *The Power of the Press: The Birth of American Political Reporting* (New York: Oxford University Press, 1986), chap. 1.

³²See David Shields, *Civil Tongues and Polite Letters in British America* (Chapel Hill: University of North Carolina, 1997); and J. A. Leo Lemay, *The Life of Benjamin Franklin* (Philadelphia: University of Pennsylvania Press, 2006), vol. 1, chap. 6. Mather is quoted in Lemay, *Life of Franklin*, 1:119. *New-England Courant*, December 4, 1721.

³³*The Papers of Benjamin Franklin*, ed. Leonard W. Larabee et al. (New Haven, CT: Yale University Press, 1958–2008), 1:13, 17, 19.

[34]Lemay, *Life of Franklin*, 1:185.

[35]Benjamin Franklin, *Benjamin Franklin's Autobiography: An Authoritative Text*, ed. J. A. Leo Lemay and P. M. Zall (New York: Norton, 1986), 14–17.

[36]Edes's career is most fully recounted in Rollo G. Silver, "Benjamin Edes: Trumpeter of Sedition," *Papers of the Bibliographical Society of America* 47 (1953): 248–68. But see also Isaiah Thomas, *The History of Printing in America* (Worcester, 1810), 1:136–39, 2:53–56; Tebbel, *Compact History*, 37–39; Joseph T. Buckingham, *Specimens of Newspaper Literature: With Personal Memoirs, Anecdotes, and Reminiscences* (Boston, 1850), 1:165–205; and Pasley, *Tyranny of Printers*, 37–40.

[37]John Eliot, *Biographical Dictionary* (Salem and Boston, 1809), 191–92; Edwin Monroe Bacon, *Boston: A Guide Book.* (Boston, 1903), 59. On Eliot, see Clifford K. Shipton, "Andrew Eliot," in *New England Life in the Eighteenth Century* (Cambridge, MA: Harvard University Press, 1963), 397–428.

[38]*New York Gazette*, August 29, 1765.

[39]John Singleton Copley to Captain R. C. Bruce, September 10, 1765, *Letters and Papers of John Singleton Copley and Henry Pelham, 1739–1776* (Boston: Massachusetts Historical Society, 1914), 36; Jennifer Roberts, "Copley's Cargo: *Boy with a Squirrel* and the Dilemma of Transit," *American Art* 21 (2007): 21–41. On Copley, see Jules Prown, *John Singleton Copley*, 2 vols. (Cambridge, MA: Harvard University Press, 1966).

[40]Burns, *Infamous Scribblers*, 353.

[41]*Works of John Adams*, 2:219.

[42]Fischer, *Paul Revere's Ride*, 53.

[43]Important critiques of popular biographies of Founding Fathers include Sean Wilentz, "America Made Easy: David McCullough, John Adams, and the Decline of Popular History," *New Republic*, July 2, 2001; and David Waldstreicher, "Founders' Chic as Culture War," *Radical History Review* 84 (Fall 2002): 185–94. See also Ray Raphael, *Founders: The People Who Brought You a Nation* (New York: Free Press, 2009); Jeffrey L. Pasley, Andrew W. Robertson, and David Waldstreicher, eds., *Beyond the Founders: New Approaches to the Political History of the Early American Republic* (Chapel Hill: University of North Carolina Press, 2004); and Gary Nash, Ray Raphael, and Alfred F. Young, eds., *Revolutionary Founders* (New York: Knopf, forthcoming). On the family feud between biographers and historians, see Jill Lepore, "Historians Who Love Too Much: Reflections on Microhistory

and Biography," *Journal of American History* 88 (June 2001): 129–44; and on a related feud between historians and novelists, see Jill Lepore, "Just the Facts, Ma'am," *New Yorker*, March 24, 2008. On history and biography in the nineteenth century, see Scott E. Casper, *Constructing American Lives: Biography and Culture in Nineteenth-Century America* (Chapel Hill: University of North Carolina Press, 1999); and Gregory M. Pfitzer, *Popular History and the Literary Marketplace, 1840–1920* (Amherst: University of Massachusetts Press, 2008).

[44] Warren, *History of the Rise, Progress, and Termination*, 1:3.

[45] Oliver Wendell Holmes, "A Ballad of the Boston Tea-Party," in *The Complete Poetical Works of Oliver Wendell Holmes* (Boston: Houghton Mifflin, 1910), 247–48.

[46] That poll is reported in Brian Stelter, "Fox Canceled Hannity's Attendance at Tea Party's Tax Day Rally in Cincinnati," *New York Times*, April 16, 2010.

[47] Arthur M. Schlesinger, "The Colonial Newspapers and the Stamp Act," *New England Quarterly* 8 (March 1935): 63–83. See also Bernard Bailyn and John B. Hench, eds., *The Press and the American Revolution* (Worcester, MA: American Antiquarian Society, 1980).

[48] Burns, *Infamous Scribblers*, 137.

[48] Schlesinger, "Colonial Newspapers," 65; Ramsay, *History*, 1:61–62.

[50] James Parker to Benjamin Franklin, June 14, 1765, *Massachusetts Historical Society Proceedings* 16 (1902): 198.

[51] The Declarations of the Stamp Act Congress, October 7–24, 1765, in Edmund S. Morgan, *Prologue to Revolution: Sources and Documents on the Stamp Act Crisis, 1764–1766* (Chapel Hill: University of North Carolina Press, 1959), 62–63.

[52] *Pennsylvania Gazette*, October 31, 1765; *Maryland Gazette*, October 10, 1765; *Connecticut Courant*, July 24, 1765. Printers' responses to the Stamp Act are also discussed in Tebbel, *Compact History*, 35–37; and in Jeffery A. Smith, *Printers and Press Freedom: The Ideology of Early American Journalism* (New York: Oxford University Press, 1988), 136–41.

[53] *New-Hampshire Gazette*, October 31, 1765; *Connecticut Courant*, July 24, 1765.

[54] *Boston Gazette*, November 11, 1765; Hannah Adams, *Summary History of New England* (Dedham, MA, 1799), 249–50.

[55] The standard account of the rise of objectivity in journalism remains Michael Schudson, *Discovering the News: A Social History of American Newspapers* (New York: Basic Books, 1978). Pasley, who

counters Schudson, offers a summary of more recent literature in *Tyranny of Printers*, chap. 1.

[56] Benjamin Franklin, "Apology for Printers," *Papers of Franklin*, 1:194–99. On Franklin's printing career, see James N. Green and Peter Stallybrass, *Benjamin Franklin: Writer and Printer* (Philadelphia: Oak Knoll Press, 2006).

[57] Coverage, tallies, and predictions include *USA Today*'s Newspaper Death Watch, 2009; Paper Cuts, http://newspaperlayoffs.com/maps/closed/; Newspaper Death Watch, http://newspaperdeathwatch.com/; Mike Doyle, "The Newspaper Is Dead, Long Live the Newspaper," *Huffington Post*, August 14, 2008; Bill Keller, "Not Dead Yet: The Newspaper in the Days of Digital Anarchy," November 29, 2007, *Guardian Weekly*, http://www.guardian.co.uk/media/2007/nov/29/pressandpublishing.digitalmedia1; and "Newspapers: Not Dead Yet?" *Seattle Times*, June 7, 2008, http://blog.seattletimes.nwsource.com/daily democracy/2008/06/newspapers_not_dead_yet.html. See also Leonard Downie Jr. and Michael Schudson, "The Reconstruction of American Journalism," *Columbia Journalism Review*, October 19, 2009, http://www.cjr.org/reconstruction/the_reconstruction_of_american.php.

Chapter 2: The Book of Ages

[1] John Adams to Benjamin Rush, April 4, 1790, Adams Papers, Letterbook, May 20, 1789–January 7, 1793, Massachusetts Historical Society, Reel 115.

[2] John Adams, *Diary and Autobiography of John Adams*, ed. L. H. Butterfield (Cambridge, MA: Harvard University Press, 1961), 1:100.

[3] John Adams to Mercy Otis Warren, July 11, 1807; Adams to Warren, July 30, 1807; Adams to Warren, August 8, 1807; Warren to Adams, August 7, 1807, in John Adams and Mercy Otis Warren, *Correspondence between John Adams and Mercy Warren*, ed. Charles Francis Adams (New York: Arno Press, 1972), 21, 381, 429, 422–23.

[4] John Adams to Timothy Pickering, August 6, 1822, *Works of John Adams*, 2:514; John Adams to Benjamin Rush, June 21, 1811, in *The Spur of Fame: Dialogues of John Adams and Benjamin Rush, 1805–1813*, ed. John A. Schultz and Douglas Adair (1966; repr., Indianapolis: Liberty Fund, 2000), 197.

[5] *John Adams*, HBO, New York, 2008.

⁶John Adams to Elbridge Gerry, April 17, 1813, in *Warren-Adams Letters* (Boston: Massachusetts Historical Society, 1925), 2:380.

⁷Jane Mecom to Benjamin Franklin, December 30, 1765; Mecom to Franklin, October 21, 1784; Franklin to Mecom, July 7, 1773; Mecom to Franklin, July 21, 1786, in *The Letters of Benjamin Franklin and Jane Mecom*, ed. Carl Van Doren (Princeton, NJ: Princeton University Press, 1950), 86, 232, 275, 139. On Mecom, see Carl Van Doren, *Jane Mecom, the Favorite Sister of Benjamin Franklin* (New York: Viking, 1950); Anne Firor Scott, *Making the Invisible Woman Visible* (Urbana: University of Illinois Press, 1984), 3–13; and Neremy A. Stern, "Jane Franklin Mecom: A Boston Woman in Revolutionary Times," *Early American Studies* 4 (2006): 147–91.

⁸Anne Bradstreet, "The Prologue," in *The Works of Anne Bradstreet*, ed. Jeannine Hensley (Cambridge, MA: Harvard University Press, 1967), 16; *Boston Evening Post*, December 10, 1744; *American Magazine, or General Repository*, August 1769, 243–44; E. Jennifer Monaghan, "Literacy Instruction and Gender in Colonial America," *American Quarterly* 40 (1988): 18–41; E. Jennifer Monaghan, *Learning to Read and Write in Colonial America* (Amherst: University of Massachusetts Press, 2005); Thomas Woody, *A History of Women's Education in the United States* (New York: Science Press, 1924), 1:146; Kenneth Lockridge, *Literacy in Colonial New England* (New York: Norton, 1974); Gloria L. Main, "An Inquiry into When and Why Women Learned to Write in Colonial New England," *Journal of Social History* 24 (Spring 1991): 579–89; Joel Perlmann and Dennis Shirley, "When Did New England Women Acquire Literacy?" *William and Mary Quarterly* 48 (1991): 50–67.

⁹Jane Mecom, "The Book of Ages" in *Letters of Franklin and Mecom*, 100–101.

¹⁰For admission and discharge records of the almshouse, see Eric Nellis and Anne Decker Cecere, eds., *The Eighteenth-Century Records of the Boston Overseers of the Poor* (Boston: Colonial Society of Massachusetts, 2007). Edward Mecom's troubles with creditors can be traced in the Suffolk Files of the Massachusetts Archives, Boston. See, for instance, *Collson v. Mecom*, January 1737, Document 45414, Reel 163; *Perkins v. Mecom*, July 1739, Document 49481, Reel 175; and *Ruddock v. Mecom*, January 1765, Document 85880, Reel 274. Jane Mecom to Deborah Franklin, September 28, 1765; Mecom to Franklin, December 30, 1765, in *Letters of Franklin and Mecom*, 83, 87. See

also *Papers of Franklin* 5:67. Jane's son Peter Franklin Mecom was the only one of her children to whom she gave a middle name.

¹¹*Papers of Franklin*, 3:306–8.

¹²Franklin to Mecom, undated but 1748, *Letters of Franklin and Mecom*, 43.

¹³Franklin to Edward and Jane Mecom, November 30, 1752, *Letters of Franklin and Mecom*, 50.

¹⁴Articles of Agreement with David Hall" [January 1, 1748], *Papers of Franklin* 3:263–67; Franklin to Mecom, June 28, 1756, *Letters of Franklin and Mecom*, 53.

¹⁵Franklin to William Strahan, April 18, 1754, *Papers of Franklin*, 5:82. See also Wilberforce Eames, *The Antigua Press and Benjamin Mecom, 1748–1765* (Worcester, MA: American Antiquarian Society, 1929).

¹⁶These transactions are recounted in notes and correspondence in *Letters of Franklin and Mecom*, 57–64.

¹⁷*Papers of Franklin*, 1:311; 2:300–301; Lemay, *Life of Franklin*, 2:172.

¹⁸*Papers of Franklin*, 3:30–31; 6:123.

¹⁹*Papers of Franklin*, 7:326–50.

²⁰Poor Richard's almanacs for 1737, 1751, 1753, 1740.

²¹*Papers of Franklin*, 7:328–29.

²²Thomas, *History of Printing*, 2:142–44.

²³Gary Nash, *The Unknown American Revolution: The Unruly Birth of Democracy and the Struggle to Create America* (New York: Viking, 2005), 62–63.

²⁴On the Butter Rebellion, see Clement Weeks, Commonplace Book containing "The Book of Harvard," c. 1772, Harvard University Archives; "Meeting of the President and Tutors," September 23, 1766, Harvard University Archives, Faculty Records III, resolution 6, 4; Samuel Eliot Morison, *Three Centuries of Harvard: 1636–1936* (Cambridge, MA: Harvard University Press, 1986), 117–18; William Coolidge Lane, *The Rebellion of 1766 in Harvard College* (Cambridge, MA: J. Wilson, 1906).

²⁵Nathaniel Appleton, *Considerations on Slavery* (Boston: Edes and Gill, 1767), 19.

²⁶Mecom to Franklin, October 23, 1767, *Letters of Franklin and Mecom*, 98; Mecom, "The Book of Ages."

²⁷Mecom to Franklin, December 1, 1767, *Letters of Franklin and Mecom*, 99; Van Doren, *Jane Mecom*, 90–91.

[28]Andrew Eliot to Thomas Hollis, September 27, 1768, in *Collections of the Massachusetts Historical Society*, 4th ser., 4 (1858): 428.

[29]Oliver Morton Dickerson, compiler, *Boston Under Military Rule, As Revealed in a Journal of the Times* (1936; repr., New York: Da Capo, 1970), 78.

[30]Benjamin West to Copley, September 10, 1768, in *Letters of Copley and Pelham*, 72.

[31]Mecom to Franklin, November 7, 1768, in *Letters of Franklin and Mecom*, 106–7.

[32]Robinson, *Wheatley*, 17.

[33]Dickerson, *Boston Under Military Rule*, 15–17.

[34]Abner Cheney Goodell, *The Trial and Execution, for Petit Treason, of Mark and Phillis* (Cambridge, 1883). On slave rebellion and the politics of fear, see Jill Lepore, *New York Burning: Liberty, Slavery and Conspiracy in Eighteenth-Century Manhattan* (New York: Knopf, 2005); Vincent Brown, *The Reaper's Garden: Death and Power in the World of Atlantic Slavery* (Cambridge, MA: Harvard University Press, 2008); and Trevor G. Burnard, *Mastery, Tyranny and Desire: Thomas Thistlewood and His Slaves in the Anglo-Jamaican World* (Chapel Hill: University of North Carolina Press, 2004).

[35]Dickerson, *Boston Under Military Rule*, 84.

[36]Ibid., 2, 21.

[37]*Works of John Adams*, 2:163, 2:226.

[38]E.g., March 16, 1770: "Mr. Otis got into a mad Freak to night & broke a great many windows in the Town House." John Rowe, *The Letters and Diary of John Rowe* (Boston, 1903), 199.

[39]Mercy Otis Warren, "A Thought on the Inestimable Blessing of Reason," in Edmund M. Hayes, "The Private Poems of Mercy Otis Warren," *New England Quarterly* 54 (1981): 213–14.

[40]Zagarri, *A Woman's Dilemma*, 52.

[41]John Trenchard, *An Argument, Shewing, that a Standing Army Is Inconsistent with a Free Government* (London, 1698), 14; Bernard Bailyn, *The Ideological Origins of the American Revolution* (Cambridge, MA: Harvard University Press, 1967), 119–20.

[42]Andrew Eliot to Thomas Hollis, September 27, 1768.

[43]*Works of John Adams*, 10:203.

[44]My account of the massacre is taken from the depositions reproduced in Frederic Kidder, *History of the Boston Massacre* (Albany, 1870). See also Hiller B. Zobel, *The Boston Massacre* (New York: Norton, 1970).

[45] *Boston Gazette*, October 2, 1750.

[46] For Wheatley, "On the Affray in King Street," see Gates, *Trials of Phillis Wheatley*, 20–21; *A Short Narrative of the Horrid Massacre in Boston* (Boston: Edes and Gill, 1770); Paul Revere, *The Bloody Massacre Perpetrated on King Street* (Boston: Edes and Gill, 1770); Henry Pelham to Paul Revere, March 29, 1770, in *Letters of Copley and Pelham*, 83.

[47] Later, Hess e-mailed me, "I work for the Government, serving the country that I love by helping it carry out its constitutionally mandated defensive functions." Austin Hess, e-mail message to the author, March 25, 2010.

[48] *The Glenn Beck Show*, Fox News, New York, May 7, 2010.

[49] Paul J. C. Friedlander, "Bicentennial Reports: Bits and Pieces," *New York Times*, November 4, 1973; Donald Bremner, "Picking up the Bicentennial Pieces," *Los Angeles Times*, July 1, 1973; J. Anthony Lukas, "Schools Turn to Negro Role in U.S.," *New York Times*, July 8, 1968; Robert Sherrill, "The Dispirit of '76: A Bicentennial Divided Against Itself," *New York Times*, March 23, 1975; John H. Fenton, "Voice of Boston's Negroes Growing Louder," *New York Times*, December 26, 1963; Malcom X, *The Autobiography of Malcolm X* (New York: Ballantine Books, 1992), 219; Bodnar, *Remaking America*, 231–32. Even the ARBA asked, reflecting on the mood in the country during the bicentennial, "what was there left to celebrate?" (ARBA, *Bicentennial of the United States of America*, 1:7). Peoples Bicentennial Commission, *America's Birthday: A Planning and Activity Guide for Citizens' Participation During the Bicentennial Years* (New York: Simon and Schuster, 1974), 9–10. On the Peoples Bicentennial Commission, see also *The Great Bicentennial Debate: History as a Political Weapon; A Record of the debate between Jeremy Rifkin and Jeffrey St. John* (Washington, DC: Heritage Foundation, 1976); Jeremy Rifkin and John Rossen, *How to Commit Revolution American Style* (Seacaucus, NJ: Lyle Stuart, 1973); Peoples Bicentennial Commission, *Voices of the Revolution* (New York: Bantam, 1974); Peoples Bicentennial Commission, *Common Sense II: The Case Against Corporate Tyranny* (New York: Bantam, 1975).

[50] Kent State posters of Revere's engraving are mentioned in Jesse Lemisch, "Radical Plot in Boston (1770): A Study in the Use of Evidence," *Harvard Law Review* 84 (1970): 504.

[51] "The View from Kent State: 11 Speak Out," *New York Times*, May 11, 1970.

[52]Howard Zinn, *You Can't Be Neutral on a Moving Train: A Personal History of Our Times* (Boston: Beacon Press, 1994), 142.

[53]Lucille Longview, interview conducted by Lenore Fenn, "Democracy and Dissent," Lexington Oral History Projects, Inc., November 18, 1992, http://www.lexingtonbattlegreen1971.com/.

[54]On the Lexington protest, see also Edward Tabor Linenthal, *Sacred Ground: Americans and Their Battlefields* (Urbana: University of Illinois Press, 1991), 40–41; "Antiwar Vets Weigh Defy of Camp Ban," *Boston Globe*, May 28, 1971; William J. Cardoso, "Antiwar Vets Camp at Concord Bridge," *Boston Globe*, May 29, 1971; Bruce McCabe, "500 Antiwar Vets Arrested on Lexington Green," *Boston Globe*, May 30, 1971; John Wood, "Antiwar Veterans March on Bunker Hill," and Joan Mahoney, "Citizens and Veterans Share Cold Night Vigil," *Boston Globe*, May 31, 1971; and "Tradition and Protests Mark Memorial Day 1971," *Spartanburg* (North Carolina) *Herald*, June 1, 1971.

[55]"The Spirit of '70: Six Historians Reflect on What Ails the American Spirit," *Newsweek*, July 6, 1970.

[56]On Hofstadter avoiding an appointment in Johnson's administration, see David S. Brown, *Richard Hofstadter: An Intellectual Biography* (Chicago: University of Chicago Press, 2006), 127–28; and Richard Hofstadter to Christopher Lasch, October 9, 1964, Richard Hofstadter Papers, Columbia University, Box 6. See also Eric Foner, "The Education of Richard Hofstadter," in *Who Owns History? Rethinking the Past in a Changing World* (New York: Hill and Wang, 2002), 25–46. Hofstadter remarked of Schlesinger, "He picks up all the troubled currents of our time and exploits them, but it is very hard to believe that he feels them, or that he feels anything very strongly but a desire to be influential and powerful." Richard Hofstadter to Daniel Aaron, undated, but probably c. 1955, Daniel Aaron Papers, Houghton Library, Harvard University, Box 17. My thanks to Daniel Aaron for permission to read these papers.

[57]Schlesinger's remarks were occasioned, in 1978, by reading the third volume of Alfred Kazin's memoirs, where this distinction was drawn. Arthur M. Schlesinger Jr., *Journals, 1952–2000*, ed. Andrew Schlesinger and Stephen Schlesinger (New York: Penguin Press, 2007), 447; Richard Hofstadter to Daniel Aaron, April 29, 1948; Daniel Aaron Papers, Houghton Library, Harvard University, Box 17.

[58]Discussions of bicentennial schlock include Jesse Lemisch, "Bicentennial Schlock," *New York Times*, October 15, 1976; and Lowenthall, "Bicentennial Landscape."

Chapter 3: How to Commit Revolution

[1]Company Overview, Historic Tours of America, courtesy of Historic Tours of America; "Boston's Best Free Map and Best Sightseeing Tour," Historic Tours of America flyer; "See the Best First! We Make Vacations Better!" Historic Tours of America flyer; "Sons and Daughters of Liberty: The Road to the American Revolution," Old Town Trolley Tours of Boston flyer, undated.

[2]*The Boston Tea Party Ships and Museum: The Story* (Key West, FL: Historic Tours of America, undated), DVD.

[3]Richard Nixon, "Second Inaugural Address: Saturday, January 20, 1973," in *Fellow Citizens*, 411.

[4]Jeremy Rifkin, "The Red, White, and Blue Left," in *How to Commit Revolution American Style: An Anthology*, ed. Jeremy Rifkin and John Rossen (Secaucus, NJ: L. Stuart, 1973), 135–36.

[5]"'76 Bicentennial Plans Cut Back as Mood Shifts," *New York Times*, July 4, 1973.

[6]Frederick Douglass, "The Meaning of July Fourth for the Negro," in *Frederick Douglass: Selected Speeches and Writings*, ed. Philip S. Foner (Chicago: Lawrence Hill Books, 1999), 196–97. Invitation to the Frederick Douglass reading, American Revolution Bicentennial Administration, Boston Regional Office, National Archives, Record Group 452, General Correspondence, Box 1.

[7]Edmund S. Morgan, *American Slavery, American Freedom: The Ordeal of Colonial Virginia* (New York: Norton, 1975); David Brion Davis, *The Problem of Slavery in the Age of Revolution, 1770–1823* (Ithaca, NY: Cornell University Press, 1975). See also Patricia Bradley, *Slavery, Propaganda and the American Revolution* (Jackson: University Press of Mississippi, 1998); David Brion Davis, *The Problem of Slavery in Western Culture* (Ithaca, NY: Cornell University Press, 1966); Peter A. Dorsey, "To 'Corroborate Our Own Claims': Public Positioning and the Slavery Metaphor in Revolutionary America," *American Quarterly* 55 (September 2003): 353–86; François Furstenberg, "Beyond Freedom and Slavery: Autonomy, Virtue, and Resistance in Early American Political Discourse," *Journal of American History* 89 (March 2003): 1295–1330; F. Nwabueze Okoye, "Chattel Slavery as the Nightmare of the American Revolutionaries," *William and Mary Quarterly* 37 (January 1980): 3–28.

[8]Nash, *Unknown American Revolution*, 119–21. On the end of slavery in England, see Adam Hochschild, *Bury the Chains: Prophets and Rebels in the Fight to Free an Empire's Slaves* (Boston: Houghton Mifflin, 2005).

[9]Mercy Otis Warren to Sarah Walter Hesilrige, c. December 1773 or March 1774, in *Selected Letters of Mercy Otis Warren*, 21–22.

[10]Henry Pelham to Copley, September 2, 1771, in *Letters of Copley and Pelham*, 150–51.

[11]Hannah Winthrop to Mercy Otis Warren, January 1, 1772, Correspondence with Mercy Otis Warren, Massachusetts Historical Society, one box.

[12]The best available collection is *The Plays and Poems of Mercy Otis Warren*, compiled by Benjamin Franklin V (Delmar, NY: Scholars' Facsimiles and Reprints, 1980).

[13]Felix to Thomas Hutchinson, January 6, 1773, and Peter Bestes, Sambo Freeman, Felix Holbrook, and Chester Joie to the Representative of the Town of Thompson, April 20, 1773, in Gary B. Nash, *Race and Revolution* (Madison, WI: Madison House, 1990), 171–74.

[14]On the portrait, see Robinson, *Wheatley*, 31–32. "To the PUBLICK," in Wheatley, *Complete Writings*, 8; Wheatley, "Farewell to America," in *Complete Writings*, 62–64; *A Forensic Dispute on the Legality of Enslaving the Africans* (Boston: John Boyle, 1773).

[15]Caesar Sartor, "Essay on Slavery," *Essex Journal and Merrimack Packet*, August 17, 1773.

[16]Wheatley, "To the Right Honourable William, Earl of Dartmouth," in *Complete Writings*, 39–40.

[17]Robinson, *Wheatley*, 39–40.

[18]Francis S. Drake, *Tea Leaves: Being a Collection of Letters and Documents* (Boston, 1884), ix.

[19]Mecom to Deborah Franklin, August 1770, in *Letters of Franklin and Mecom*, 114.

[20]Phillis Wheatley to David Worcester, October 18, 1773, in *Complete Writings*, 146–47.

[21]"Tea Is Brewing: A Guide for Teachers" (Boston: Old South Meeting House, 2009).

[22]Ralph Waldo Emerson, "Boston," in *Complete Works*, 9:215.

[23]Young, *Shoemaker*, 187.

[24]Ronald P. Formisiano, *Boston Against Busing: Race, Class and Ethnicity in the 1960s and 1970s* (Chapel Hill: University of North Carolina Press, 1991), 281 n. 19; Boston Public Schools Report on

Teaching and Learning, 2008, http://www.bostonpublicschools.org/files/reportcards/SCH4340.pdf.

[25]In 2010, the tea Melvill found in his shoes remained on display at the Old State House. The chest was purchased by Historic Tours of America in 2005. "Historic Tours of America Acquires Rare Tea Chest from Boston Tea Party," press release, January 5, 2005, http://www.bostonteapartyship.com/pressrelease.asp.

[26]Paul J. C. Friedlander, "Bicentennial Reports: Bits and Pieces," *New York Times*, November 4, 1973; Donald Bremner, "Picking up the Bicentennial Pieces," *Los Angeles Times*, July 1, 1973.

[27]"An Editorial: The Boston Tea Party . . . and this Generation," *Boston Globe*, December 10, 1973. The next day, Nixon signed a bill creating the American Revolution Bicentennial Administration, granting it far greater powers than the defunct commission.

[28]Georgia Ireland to Lewis A. Carter, February 13, 1974, American Revolution Bicentennial Administration, Boston Regional Office, National Archives, Record Group 452, Box 1.

[29]Peter Anderson, "Faneuil Hall Rally Urged to Demand Impeachment," December 17, 1973; [Sarasota Florida] *Herald Tribune*, December 17, 1973.

[30]J. Anthony Lukas, *Common Ground: A Turbulent Decade in the Life of Three American Families* (New York: Knopf, 1985), 316.

[31]Lewis A. Carter Jr. to Georgia Ireland, January 25, 1974, American Revolution Bicentennial Administration, Boston Regional Office, National Archives, Record Group 452, Box 1.

[32]"'Tea Party' Won't Be Forgotten Soon," *Atlanta Journal*, December 17, 1973; Joseph Rosenbloom and David Richwine, "Rebels Steal Tea Party Show, 'Dump' Oil," *Boston Globe*, December 17, 1973.

[33]Lewis A. Carter Jr. to Georgia Ireland, January 25, 1974. Photographs of the reenactment and the protest are reproduced in ARBA, *Bicentennial of the United States of America*, 1:106–9.

[34]Stephen Isaacs, "Boston Tea Party Restaged," *Washington Post*, December 17, 1973.

[35]Peoples Bicentennial Commission, *America's Birthday*, chap. 3.

[36]Peoples Bicentennial Commission, *Common Sense II*, front matter.

[37]"Boston Just Say No Party," *Boston Globe*, July 16, 1988; Bruce Butterfield, "Labor Has Its Day," *Boston Globe*, September 8, 1992; Dolores Kong, "Doctors and Nurses Plan to Protest at Tea Party Ship," *Boston Globe*, December 1, 1997; Aaron Zitner, "Tax Code Foes Find

Nation Indifferent," *Boston Globe*, April 16, 1998; April Simpson, "Legislators Dump U.S. Mandates," *Boston Globe*, August 6, 2007.

[38] *Works of John Adams*, 3:323; 9:335; Mercy Otis Warren, "The Squabble of the Sea Nymphs," in *Plays and Poems*, 202–5.

[39] John Hancock, *An Oration Delivered March 5, 1774* (Newport, 1774), 9.

[40] Young, *Shoemaker*, part 2.

[41] Daniel Webster, "The Bunker Hill Monument, An Address delivered . . . on the Seventeenth of June, 1825," in *Daniel Webster's First Bunker Hill Oration*, ed. Fred Newton Scott (New York, 1902), 25.

[42] Holmes, "The Last Leaf," in *Complete Poetical Works*, 1–2.

[43] Herman Melville, *Israel Potter* (New York, 1855), 51, 272–76.

[44] Young, *Shoemaker*, 121–79.

[45] A Citizen of New York [James Hawkes], *A Retrospect of the Boston Tea-Party: With a Memoir of George R. T. Hewes* (New York, 1834); Young, *Shoemaker*, 3–6. See also A Bostonian [Benjamin Bussey Thatcher], *Traits of the Tea Party: Being a Memoir of George R. T. Hewes* (New York, 1835).

[46] Fischer, *Paul Revere's Ride*, 51.

[47] John Morgan to Isaac Jamieux, November 24, 1773, in *Letters of Copley and Pelham*, 210.

[48] *Works of Adams*, 2:367.

[49] Craig Nelson, *Thomas Paine: Enlightenment, Revolution, and the Birth of Modern Nations* (New York: Viking, 2006), 49.

[50] Warren, *History of the Rise, Progress, and Termination*, 1:87.

[51] Josiah Quincy, *Memoir of the Life of Josiah Quincy Jun.* (Boston, 1875), 363.

[52] Nathaniel Niles, *Two Discourses on Liberty* (Newburyport, 1774), 38.

[53] Petition from "a Grate Number of Blackes" to Thomas Gage, May 25, 1774, Jeremy Belknap Papers, Massachusetts Historical Society, Box 3.

[54] Abigail Adams to John Adams, September 22, 1774, *Adams Family Correspondence*, ed. L. H. Butterfield et al. (Cambridge, MA: Harvard University Press, 1963–93), 1:161–62.

[55] Samuel Johnson, *Taxation No Tyranny* (London, 1775), 89.

[56] Phillis Wheatley to Samson Occom, February 11, 1774, in *Complete Writings*, 152–53.

[57] Simon Schama, *Rough Crossings: Britain, the Slaves, and the American Revolution* (New York: HarperCollins, 2005), 8. See also Cassandra Pybus, *Epic Journeys of Freedom: Runaway Slaves of the*

American Revolution and their Global Quest for Liberty (Boston: Beacon Press, 2006); and Woody Holton, *Forced Founders: Indians, Debtors, Slaves, and the Making of the American Revolution* (Chapel Hill: University of North Carolina Press, 1999).

[58] Austin Hess, e-mail message to the author, April 26, 2010.

[59] Polls were conducted in 2010 by CBS News / New York Times, Quinnipiac University Polling Institute, the Pew Research Center, and *USA Today*. "The Tea Party Movement: What They Think," CBS News and the *New York Times*, poll, April 5–12, 2010; "Quinnipiac University Poll," Quinnipiac University Polling Institute, poll, March 24, 2010; "The People and Their Government: Distrust, Discontent, Anger and Partisan Rancor," Pew Research Center for the People and the Press, poll, April 18, 2010, http://www.gallup.com/poll/127181/tea-partiers-fairly-mainstream-demographics.aspx.

[60] On the Lost Cause of the Confederacy in American history and memory, see Tony Horwitz, *Confederates in the Attic: Dispatched from the Unfinished Civil War* (New York: Pantheon, 1998); and David W. Blight, *Race and Reunion: The Civil War in American Memory* (Cambridge, MA: Harvard University Press, 2001).

[61] *The Glenn Beck Show*, Fox News, New York, January 13, 2010.

[62] Austin Hess, e-mail message to the author, April 26, 2010.

Chapter 4: The Past upon Its Throne

[1] David S. Bernstein, "Tea Is for Terrorism," *Boston Phoenix*, April 8, 2010.

[2] Tuerck at the Boston Common Tea Party rally, April 15, 2009; Boston Tea Party 2009, weblog, April 22, 2009, http://teapartyboston2009.blogspot.com/; Ridpath at the Boston Common Tea Party rally, July 4, 2009; John Ridpath, "John Ridpath at the July 4 Boston Tea Party Protest."

[3] [Boston] *Weekly Dig*, April 7, 2010.

[4] Fischer, *Paul Revere's Ride*, 76–77.

[5] Silver, "Benjamin Edes," 261.

[6] Paul Revere to Jeremy Belknap, January 1, 1798, in *Proceedings of the Massachusetts Historical Society* 16 (1878): 371–76.

[7] Samuel Lane Boardman, ed., *Peter Edes: A Biography, with His Diary* (Bangor, 1901), 8; Silver, "Benjamin Edes," 262.

[8] Gross, *Minutemen and Their World*, chap. 5; James Russell Lowell, "Lines Suggested by the Graves of Two English Soldiers on

Concord Battle-Ground," in *The Complete Poetical Works of James Russell Lowell* (Boston: Houghton Mifflin, 1896), 97.

[9]Van Doren, *Jane Mecom*, 118, 124–34; Franklin to Mecom, October 16, 1775, *Letters of Franklin and Mecom*, 164.

[10]Andrew Eliot to Thomas Hollis, April 25, 1775, Andrew Eliot to John Eliot, May 4, 1775, *Proceedings of the Massachusetts Historical Society* 16 (1878): 281–82.

[11]Henry Pelham to John Singleton, May 16, 1775, in *Letters of Copley and Pelham*, 318; Boardman, *Peter Edes*, 99.

[12]Silver, "Benjamin Edes," 262; Morison, *Three Centuries of Harvard*, 148–51.

[13]Raphael, *Founding Myths*, chap. 9.

[14]Andrew Eliot Annotated Almanacs, Massachusetts Historical Society, Box 2. Eliot kept his diary for 1775 interleaved in the pages of Nathanael Low, *An Astronomical Diary: Or, Almanack, for the Year . . . 1775* (Boston, n.d.).

[15]James Russell Lowell, "Under the Old Elm," in *Complete Poetical Works*, 364–70.

[16]Spencer Albright, *The American Ballot* (Washington, DC: American Council on Public Affairs, 1942), 16. On peas and beans in use in sixteenth- and seventeenth-century England, see Charles Gross, "The Early History of the Ballot in England," *American Historical Review* 3 (April 1898): 458–59. On voting behavior, see Robert J. Dinkin, *Voting in Provincial America: A Study of Elections in the Thirteen Colonies, 1689–1776* (Westport, CT: Greenwood Press, 1977). See also Robert J. Dinkin, ed., *Election Day: A Documentary History* (Westport, CT: Greenwood Press, 2002), 1–27, 47–60.

[17]Albright, *American Ballot*, 14–15.

[18]*Records of the Federal Convention of 1787*, ed. Max Farrand (New Haven, CT: Yale University Press, 1911), 2:240–41.

[19]Waldstreicher, *Slavery's Constitution*, 81, 83, 85, 103, 104. See also François Furstenberg, *In the Name of the Father: Washington's Legacy, Slavery, and the Making of a Nation* (New York: Penguin, 2006); and Harry Wiencek, *An Imperfect God: George Washington, His Slaves, and the Creation of America* (New York: Farrar, Strauss, and Giroux, 2003).

[20]As Waldstreicher has argued, "In the new American order, taxation with representation and slavery were joined at the hip" (*Slavery's Constitution*, 5).

[21]On the history of suffrage, see Alexander Keyssar, *The Right to Vote: The Contested History of Democracy in the United States* (New York: Basic Books, 2000).

[22]Douglas Campbell, "The Origin of American Institutions, as Illustrated in the History of the Written Ballot," *Papers of the American Historical Association* 4 (1891): 179.

[23]Robert J. Dinkin, *Voting in Revolutionary America: A Study of Elections in the Original Thirteen States* (Westport, CT: Greenwood Press, 1982), 102.

[24]See Keyssar, *Right to Vote*; and Sean Wilentz, *The Rise of American Democracy: Jefferson to Lincoln* (New York: Norton, 2005).

[25]Richard Bensel, *The American Ballot Box in the Mid-Nineteenth Century* (Cambridge: Cambridge University Press, 2004).

[26]*Henshaw v. Foster et al.*, 26 Mass. 312 (1830).

[27]L. E. Fredman, *The Australian Ballot: The Story of an American Reform* (Lansing: Michigan State University Press, 1968), 22, 28; Bensel, *American Ballot Box*, 15.

[28]William M. Ivins, *Machine Politics and Money in Elections in New York City* (New York: Harper, 1887), 56–57, 63–64.

[29]Frank O'Gorman, "The Secret Ballot in Nineteenth-Century Britain," in *Cultures of Voting: The Hidden History of the Secret Ballot*, ed. Romain Bertrand et al. (London: Hurst, 2007), 22–23.

[30]John Crowley, "Uses and Abuses of the Secret Ballot in the American Age of Reform," in *Cultures of Voting*, 52.

[31]Michael Brunet, "The Secret Ballot Issue in Massachusetts Politics from 1851 to 1853," *New England Quarterly* 25 (September 1952): 354–62.

[32]Fredman, *Australian Ballot*, 8; John Henry Wigmore, *The Australian Ballot System* (Boston, 1889); Philip Loring Allen, "Ballot Laws and Their Workings," *Political Science Quarterly* 21 (March 1906): 38–58. On the early consequences, see Jerrold G. Rusk, "The Effect of the Australian Ballot Reform on Split Ticket Voting: 1876–1908," *American Political Science Review* 64 (December 1970): 1220–38.

[33]Crowley, "Uses and Abuses," 59.

[34]Carl Becker, *The Heavenly City of Eighteenth-Century Philosophers* (New Haven, CT: Yale University Press, 1963).

[35]James Madison, Alexander Hamilton, and John Jay, *The Federalist Papers*, ed. Isaac Kramnick (New York: Penguin Books, 1987), 144.

[36]Herman Melville, *Typee, Oomo, Mardi* (New York: Library of America, 1982), 1169–70.

[37]George Levesque, *Black Boston: African American Life and Culture in Urban America, 1750–1860* (New York: Garland, 1994), 165.

[38]On Crispus Attucks Day, Attucks, Wheatley, Bunker Hill, and slavery in history and memory, see Margot Minardi, "'The Inevitable

Negro': Making Slavery History in Massachusetts, 1770–1863" (Ph.D. diss., Harvard University, 2007).

[39]Theodore Parker, "On the Boston Kidnapping," in *The Collected Works of Theodore Parker*, ed. Frances Power Cobb (London, 1863), 5:209–10.

[40]William E. Cain, ed., *William Lloyd Garrison and the Fight Against Slavery* (Boston: Bedford/St. Martin's, 1995), 35–36.

[41]Burns's speech appeared in the *Liberator*, March 9, 1855.

[42]Anthony Burns to the Baptist Church, undated but November or December 1855, in Charles Emery Stevens, *Anthony Burns: A History* (Boston, 1856), 280–83.

[43]William Cooper Nell, *The Colored Patriots of the American Revolution* (Boston, 1855), 5.

[44]Paul Finkelman, ed., *Dred Scott v. Sandford: A Brief History with Documents* (Boston: Bedford/St. Martin's, 1997), 149.

[45]Abraham Lincoln and Stephen Douglas, *The Lincoln-Douglas Debates: The First Complete, Unexpurgated Text*, ed. Harold Holzer (New York: HarperCollins, 1993), 54, 252.

[46]James Ayres, "Busing Foes Take Their Protest to Replay of Boston Massacre," *Boston Globe*, March 6, 1975; Lukas, *Common Ground*, 315–17.

[47]"Text of President Ford's Address in Old North Church," and Nina McCain, "Historian Hits Buildup of Presidential Power," *Boston Globe*, April 19, 1975.

[48]Gary McMillan, "'Peoples' Rally Jams Concord," and John B. Wood and Curtis Wilkie, "Ford Opens Bicentennial Events Here," *Boston Globe*, April 19, 1975.

[49]"Now Is the Time for Reconciliation, Not Rancor"; Ken Hartenit, "President Gets Cheers, Boos"; Peter Anderson, "Protest, Pomp at Concord Bridge"; Stephen Wermiel, "Ford Appeals for National Unity, Ignores Concord Protesters' Boos"; Gary McMillan, "Rally More Like a Party with Raspberry for Ford," *Boston Globe*, April 20, 1976.

[50]Lukas, *Common Ground*, 317.

[51]On *Brown v. Board of Education*, see Michael Klarman, *From Jim Crow to Civil Rights: The Struggle for Racial Equality* (Oxford: Oxford University Press, 2004). On originalism, see Jack N. Rakove, *Original Meanings: Politics and Ideas in the Making of the Constitution* (New York: Knopf, 1996), especially chap. 1; and Stephen M. Griffin, *American Constitutionalism: From Theory to Politics* (Princeton, NJ: Princeton University Press, 1996), especially chap. 5.

[52] Thurgood Marshall, *Thurgood Marshall: His Speeches, Writings, Arguments, Opinions, and Reminiscences*, ed. Mark V. Tushnet (Chicago: Lawrence Hill Books, 2001), 281–85.

[53] Jerry Falwell, *Listen America!* (Garden City, NJ: Doubleday, 1980), 29; Tim LaHaye, *The Faith of Our Founding Fathers* (Brentwood, TN: Wolgemuth and Hyatt, 1987), 1, 5, 13, 115–16.

[54] Benjamin Franklin, *Works of the Late Dr. Benjamin Franklin* (New Haven, 1797), 84.

[55] On these documents, see Martha Nussbaum, *Liberty of Conscience: In Defense of America's Tradition of Religious Equality* (New York: Basic Books, 2008). Mitt Romney, "Faith in America," NPR, December 6, 2007, http://www.npr.org/templates/story/story.php?story Id=16969460.

[56] Frank Lambert, *The Founding Fathers and the Place of Religion in America* (Princeton, NJ: Princeton University Press, 2003).

Chapter 5: Your Superexcellent Age

[1] Richard J. Ellis, *To the Flag: The Unlikely History of the Pledge of Allegiance* (Lawrence: University of Kansas Press, 2005). Ellis discusses Francis Bellamy in chapters 1 and 2, recounts the insertion of "under God" in chapter 5, and relates the story of the Dukakis veto in chapter 6. Edward Bellamy, *Looking Backward, 2000–1887*, ed. Daniel H. Borus (Boston: Bedford Books, 1995), 48; Bodnar, *Remaking America*, 232, 237; Lukas, *Common Ground*, 317.

[2] Thomas Paine, *The Complete Writings of Thomas Paine*, ed. Philip Foner (New York: Citadel Press, 1945), 1:3, 17.

[3] John Adams, *Papers of John Adams*, ed. Robert J. Taylor (Cambridge, MA: Harvard University Press, 1977), 4:37, 41, 53, 29. On Paine, see especially Eric Foner, *Tom Paine and Revolutionary America* (New York: Oxford University Press, 1976).

[4] *Writings of Paine*, 1:19.

[5] *Diary and Autobiography of John Adams*, 3:330–41.

[6] Phillis Wheatley to George Washington, October 26, 1775, and George Washington to Phillis Wheatley, February 28, 1776, in *Complete Writings*, 160.

[7] Van Doren, *Jane Mecom*, 128.

[8] Andrew Eliot to Isaac Smith Jr., April 5, 1776, in George E. Ellis, *March 17th, 1876: Celebration of the Centennial Anniversary of the*

Evacuation of Boston by the British . . . and a Chronicle of the Siege of Boston (Boston: City Council, 1876), 190–92.

[9]Van Doren, *Jane Mecom*, 130.

[10]Abigail Adams to John Adams, July 14, 1776, in *The Letters of John and Abigail Adams*, ed. Frank Shuffelton (New York: Penguin, 204), 200.

[11]*New England Chronicle*, July 15, 1776.

[12]Pybus, *Epic Journeys*, 9–12.

[13]Klein, "Commemorating the American Revolution," 258, 260.

[14]Klarman, *From Jim Crow*, 428.

[15]Arthur M. Schlesinger Jr., *Robert Kennedy and His Times* (Boston: Houghton Mifflin, 1978, 2002), 234.

[16]*The Attempt to Steal the Bicentennial, Peoples Bicentennial Commission, Report of the Subcommittee of the . . . Committee on the Judiciary* (Washington, DC: Government Printing Office, 1976).

[17]"The Great Celebration," *Washington Post*, July 7, 1976. See also ARBA, *Bicentennial of the United States of America*, 1:17, 51.

[18]Louis P. Masur, *The Soiling of Old Glory: The Story of a Photograph that Shocked America* (New York: Bloomsbury, 2008).

[19]Robert Lowell, "For the Union Dead," in *Collected Poems*, ed. Frank Bidart and David Gewanter (New York: Farrar, Strauss, and Giroux, 2003), 377.

[20]*Writings of Paine*, 1:49–50; Nelson, *Thomas Paine*, 108.

[21]Shipton, *New England Life*, 425–27.

[22]Van Doren, *Jane Mecom*, 132–33.

[23]Mecom to Franklin, August 15, 1778, and Mecom to Franklin, February 14, 1779, in *Letters of Franklin and Mecom*, 184, 188–89.

[24]Gross, *Minutemen and Their World*, 136.

[25]Robinson, *Wheatley*, 52–64.

[26]Schama, *Rough Crossings*; Pybus, *Epic Journeys*, 8.

[27]Graham Russell Hodges, ed., *The Black Loyalist Directory: African Americans in Exile After the American Revolution* (New York: Garland, 1995), 111.

[28]Pybus, *Epic Journeys*, 150, 182; Schama, *Rough Crossings*, 310–11, 328, 390, 394–95.

[29]Waldstreicher, *Slavery's Constitution*, 49–50.

[30]Minardi, "'The Inevitable Negro'"; Joanne Pope Melish, *Disowning Slavery: Gradual Emancipation and 'Race' in New England, 1780–1860* (Ithaca, NY: Cornell University Press, 1998); and John Wood Sweet, *Bodies Politic: Negotiating Race in the American North, 1730–1830* (Baltimore: Johns Hopkins University Press, 2003).

[31]Tudor, *Life of Otis*, 485; Buckingham, *Specimens*, 197; Silver, "Benjamin Edes," 264–65; John Keane, *Tom Paine: A Political Life* (Boston: Little, Brown, 1985), xiii; Jane Mecom to Benjamin Franklin, January 17, 1790, *Letters of Franklin and Mecom*, 338.

[32]Mark Twain, "The Late Benjamin Franklin," *Galaxy* 10 (1870): 138–40.

[33]*Poor Richard's Almanack*, 1736.

[34]*Writings of Paine*, 1:286, 344, 404–5.

[35]Nelson, *Thomas Paine*, 248, 274–75, 281.

[36]*Writings of Paine*, 1:464, 599; Harvey J. Kaye, *Thomas Paine and the Promise of America* (New York: Hill and Wang, 2005), 171; Samuel Adams to Thomas Paine, November 30, 1802, in *The Writings of Samuel Adams*, ed. Harry Alonzo Cushing (New York: G. P. Putnam's Sons, 1908), 4:412.

[37]*Massachusetts Mercury*, May 19, 1794.

[38]Pasley, *Tyranny of Printers*, 33, and app. 2.

[39]On the press in the 1790s, see both Pasley and Marcus Daniel, *Scandal and Civility: Journalism and the Birth of American Democracy* (New York: Oxford University Press, 2009).

[40]James Morton Smith, *Freedom's Fetters: The Alien and Sedition Laws and American Civil Liberties* (Ithaca, NY: Cornell University Press, 1956); Leonard W. Levy, *Emergence of a Free Press* (New York: Oxford University Press, 1985).

[41]Silver, "Benjamin Edes," 265–68.

[42]Garry Wills, *"Negro President": Jefferson and the Slave Power* (Boston: Houghton Mifflin, 2003), 2.

[43]Thomas Jefferson, "First Inaugural Address: Wednesday, March 4, 1801," in *Fellow Citizens*, 23; Probate Records of Boston Printers, 1803–1824, Massachusetts Historical Society, one box; Probate Inventory of Benjamin Edes, June 23, 1801.

[44]Paul Collins, *The Trouble with Tom: The Strange Afterlife and Times of Thomas Paine* (New York: Bloomsbury, 2005), 15.

[45]*Diary and Autobiography of John Adams*, 3:330–41.

[46]Collins, *Trouble with Tom*, 29.

[47]*Works of John Adams*, 10:381.

[48]Robert L. Brunhouse, ed., "David Ramsay, 1749–1815 Selections from His Writings," *Transactions of the American Philosophical Society* 55 (1965): 27.

[49]Warren, *History of the Rise, Progress, and Termination*, 1:379.

[50]Raphael, *Founding Myths*, chap. 1.

[51] Foner, *Tom Paine and Revolutionary America*, 257.

[52] The Peoples Bicentennial Commission, *Common Sense II*; Glenn Beck and Joe Kerry, *Common Sense: The Case Against an Out-of-Control Government* (New York: Threshold Editions, 2009).

[53] *The Glenn Beck Show*, Fox News, New York, February 18, 2010.

[54] The fate of those bones is Collins's subject in *Trouble with Tom*.

[55] G. Thomas Tansell, *Royall Tyler* (Cambridge, MA: Harvard University Press, 1967), 11–12; and Royall Tyler, *The Algerine Captive; Or, The Life and Adventures of Doctor Updike Underhill*, ed. Caleb Crain (1797; repr., New York: Modern Library, 2002), xx–xxii.

[56] Royall Tyler, *The Contrast: A Comedy in Five Acts*, with a history of George Washington's copy by James Benjamin Wilbur (1790; repr., Boston: Houghton Mifflin, 1920); Tyler, *Algerine Captive*, xxvi.

[57] [Royall Tyler], *The Origin of Evil: An Elegy* (n.p., 1793).

[58] Royall Tyler, *The Prose of Royall Tyler*, ed. Marius B. Péladaut (Montpelier: Vermont Historical Society, 1972), 178, 185. See also *The Verse of Royall Tyler*, ed. Marius B. Péladaut (Charlottesville: University of Virginia Press, 1968). On Mary Tyler, see Mary Tyler, *Grandmother Tyler's Book: The Recollections of Mary Palmer Tyler, 1775–1866*, ed. Frederick Tupper and Helen Tyler Brown (New York: G. P. Putnam's Sons, 1925); and see Mary Tyler, *The Maternal Physician: A Treatise on the Nature and Management of Infants* (Philadelphia, 1818).

[59] "Paine's religious opinions were those of three-fourths of the men of letters of the last age," Joel Barlow observed, overstating the case, if not by much. "Plea for a Patriot," *Galaxy* 21 (May 1876): 593.

[60] Tyler, *Algerine Captive*, 128–36.

[61] Paul Baepler, ed., introduction to *White Slaves, African Masters: An Anthology of American Barbary Captivity Narratives* (Chicago: University of Chicago Press, 1999).

[62] "Treaty of Peace and Friendship between the United States of America and the Bey and Subjects of Tripoli, of Barbary," in United States, *Laws of the United States of America* (Philadelphia, 1804), 4:46.

[63] Royall Tyler, *The Touchstone; Or a Humble Modest Inquiry into the Nature of Religious Intolerance*. The manuscript has since been lost, and only the first thirty pages of the unfinished printing survive. My thanks to the University of Vermont for sending me a copy of the incomplete printing. *Prose of Royall Tyler*, 352–53.

[64] *Prose of Royall Tyler*, 43–44.

Epilogue: Revering America

[1]All quotations from and descriptions of the April 18, 2010, Revere America rally, as well as information on the organization, are taken from the RevereAmerica.org website, http://revereamerica.org/; Van Doren, *Jane Mecom*, 239.

[2]Mecom to Franklin, July 21, 1786, *Letters of Franklin and Mecom*, 275.

[3]Franklin, *Autobiography*, 1.

[4]Monaghan, "Literacy Instruction and Gender," 27; Woody, *History of Women's Education*, 146.

[5]Longfellow, "Paul Revere's Ride."

[6]State of Arizona Senate, *Support Our Law Enforcement and Safe Neighborhoods Act of 2010*, State of Arizona Senate Resolution 1070, 49th legislature, 2nd reg. sess., April 23, 2010; Randal C. Archibold, "Arizona Enacts Stringent Law on Immigration," *New York Times*, April 24, 2010.

[7]Christen Varley, "MA House Vote on Perry's Illegal Immigration Amendment," Greater Boston Tea Party, May 2, 2010, http://greaterbostonteaparty.com/2010/05/ma-house-vote-on-perrys-illegal-immigration-amendment/; Christen Varley, "'Pass the Perry Amendment' Rally," Greater Boston Tea Party, May 19, 2010, http://greaterbostonteaparty.com/2010/05/pass-the-perry-amendment-rally/; Maria Sacchetti, "Tea Party Rally Calls for Senate Amendment on Illegal Immigrants," *Boston Globe*, May 21, 2010.

[8]Massachusetts State Congress, *Massachusetts State Congress Journal*, 186th sess., April 28, 2010, 3–6; Massachusetts State Congress, *An Act Relative to Public Benefits*, H.R. 3387, 186th sess., January 7, 2009.

[9]Glenn Beck, *The Glenn Beck Show*, Fox News, New York, April 30, 2010.

[10]Glenn Beck, *The Glenn Beck Show*, Fox News, New York, May 7, 2010.

[11]Bill O'Reilly, *The O'Reilly Factor*, Fox News, New York, May 7, 2010.

[12]Langston Hughes, "Let America Be America Again," in *The Collected Poems of Langston Hughes*, ed. Arnold Rampersad (New York: Knopf, 1998), 189.

[13]Organization of American Historians Executive Board of Directors, "Texas Textbook Resolution," Organization of American Historians, May 12, 2010, http://www.oah.org/news/20100512_texas_textbook_resolution.html.

[14]E.g., letter from Fritz Fischer, chair, National Council for History Education, to the Texas State Board of Education, National Council for History Education, Inc., March 30, 2010, http://www.nche.net/includes/downloads/nchelettertotexas.pdf.

[15]Jonathan J. Cooper, "Arizona Governor Signs Bill Targeting Ethnic Studies," Associated Press, May 12, 2010.

[16]Cynthia Dunbar, "A Christian Land Governed by Christian Principles," Texas State Board of Education meeting, video clip, Texas Freedom Network, YouTube, May 21, 2010, http://www.youtube.com/watch?v=AdhGK9aYjDY.

[17]Michael Brick, "Texas School Board Set to Vote Textbook Revisions," New York Times, May 21, 2010; "Benjamin Todd Jealous Testimony Before Texas Board of Education," video clip, NAACP Videos, YouTube, May 20, 2010, http://www.youtube.com/watch?v=qQ_T3Z3y4n8.

[18]Rachel Maddow, The Rachel Maddow Show, MSNBC, New York, May 19, 2010; Adam Nagourney and Carl Hulse, "Tea Party Pick Causes Uproar on Civil Rights," New York Times, May 20, 2010; "Tea Party Candidate Causes Civil Rights Stir," New York Times, May 21, 2010.

INDEX

The Public Square Book Series
PRINCETON UNIVERSITY PRESS

With thanks to the donors of the Public Square

President William P. Kelly,
the CUNY Graduate Center

President Jeremy Travis,
John Jay College of Criminal Justice

Myron S. Glucksman

Caroline Urvater